Butchering Small Game and Birds

Rabbits, Hares, Poultry
and Wild Birds

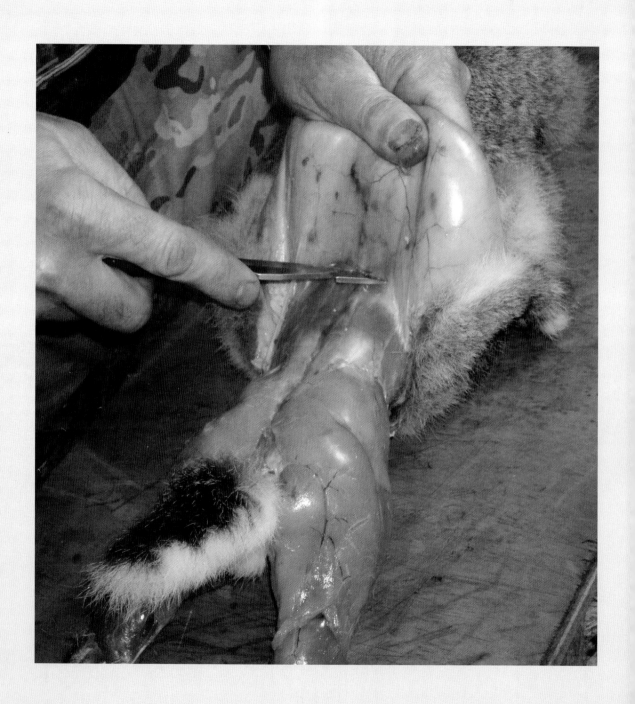

Butchering Small Game and Birds

Rabbits, Hares, Poultry and Wild Birds

John Bezzant

THE CROWOOD PRESS

First published in 2012 by
The Crowood Press Ltd
Ramsbury, Marlborough
Wiltshire SN8 2HR

www.crowood.com

British Library Cataloguing-in-Publication Data
A catalogue record for this book is available from the British Library.

ISBN 978 1 84797 423 5

Disclaimer
The author and the publisher do not accept any responsibility in any manner whatsoever for any error or omission, or any loss, damage, injury, adverse outcome, or liability of any kind incurred as a result of the use of any of the information contained in this book, or reliance upon it. If in doubt about any aspect of the butchery of small game and birds, readers are advised to seek professional advice.

Please note that if you intend to sell meat that you have butchered to the general public, there are numerous regulations to be followed, and you should contact your local environmental health department for advice. However, for the smallholder or private individual wishing to butcher small game or birds there are no restrictions or legal obligations other than the fact that if you were to cause undue suffering to an animal or bird during slaughter you would, of course, be causing animal cruelty would be liable to prosecution.

Typeset by Bookcraft Ltd, Stroud, Gloucestershire
Printed and bound in Malaysia by Times Offset (M) Sdn Bhd

Contents

Introduction

The skilful butchering of small game and birds is not a magical art reserved for a chosen few, but a craft that can be learnt by any individual willing to master the basic techniques involved. However, you must first answer a question of utmost importance: are you the sort of person who can carry out butchery tasks? The beginning of the butchering process is the killing of an animal; in many cases the killing will be carried out at close quarters, using your bare hands. Obviously this is not something that everybody can do and there is no shame in that. Therefore, the first tool that you require is the kind of detached nature that means you can kill a small, furry animal that you have reared yourself, such as a rabbit or a bird, which you may have become fond of.

We will look at this aspect in much more detail in Chapter 2; however, I have posed the question regarding your suitability for butchering tasks at this early stage so that you can think about it seriously before I start to introduce you to the nitty gritty of slaughtering small animals and birds. You also need to have a strong stomach that does not become queasy at the sight of blood or entrails, as it goes without saying that the butchering of small animals or birds will bring you face to face with both these bodily components.

Butchering is a very earthy, fundamental craft that, when skilfully performed, is very satisfying. However, a person who is squeamish will be hesitant which will, in turn, lead to a poorly performed butchery job, with the ruination of nutritious meat, meaning that an animal has died unnecessarily. So you see, the most important tool of all is, in fact, yourself: if you have the right frame of mind and a strong stomach, then all the skills you require to become a competent butcher of small game and birds can be learnt from the following pages. There is no need for a short course or for anybody to give you tuition; the skills required are very straightforward and it is perfectly possible for you to teach yourself.

I have taken an abundance of photos to help explain every single stage in fine detail, so there is a lot to read and much to look at, but if you study it closely you will soon become a very competent home butcher of small game and birds. I say home butcher because you can never hope to become a professional butcher; they are skilled men who undergo extensive training, followed by daily practice of their craft, so, although you will become a competent practitioner of the butchering craft, you will not quite match the standards of a professional. The work of the professional may be that bit finer than the work of the home butcher, but the home butcher can still produce a very fine carcase that is hygienic, well presented and cooks well, which is all that matters.

The amateur butcher can produce a very presentable carcase.

Killing birds that you have reared yourself, that you may have become fond of, is not an undertaking to be entered into lightly.

chapter one

Tools of the Trade

KNIVES

Knives are the most important item of your butchery kit; other items may be dispensed with, their use simply making the job easier and the finished product finer, but the knife is essential – without it you simply cannot carry out the butchering of small game or birds. You can get away with just one knife if absolutely necessary, but it is far better to have a number, each one performing a specific task.

Price is not an indicator of a knife's usability; I have owned some very cheap knives that performed their task admirably and owned expensive knives that were next to useless. The first requirement of a good knife is that it feels comfortable in the hand; we all have hands of

different shapes and sizes and what fits well into the bear-sized fist of a large man, will not fit as comfortably in the more delicate hand of a small woman. For this reason it is best to buy your knives from a local outlet, rather than over the internet, as you need to test the knife for its feel, prior to purchase. Remember, if the cheaper knife feels more comfortable than the expensive one, go for the cheaper option, even if the more expensive knife has a finer quality blade. The cheaper blade will actually do a better job if the fit of the haft is the more comfortable, for the simple reason that you will be better able to control and manipulate the blade.

Much has been written about the material from which the haft of a knife is made; the selection includes: natural wood, horn and a

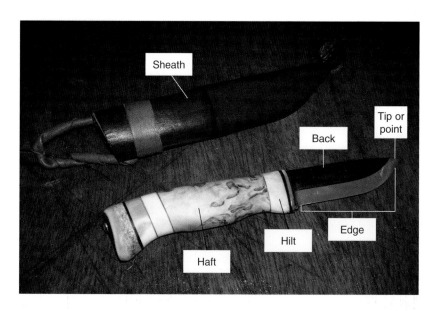

The points of the knife.

whole range of plastics. The concern often raised over smooth handles, such as wood, is that when a hand becomes slippery (when bloody for example) it can slip down the haft into contact with the sharp blade. The hand can indeed slip on a smooth haft, but it should not happen: one of the basic rules of butchering is to keep the hands clean at all times, if they become bloody or greasy then you halt operations and wash them. A professional butcher when asked what was the secret of good butchery answered: 'Clean hands'. Clean hands are better able to control the tools of the trade, whereas dirty, blooded and greasy hands will never be in full control of the implements.

In the field, where it could be raining and muddy and where it is impossible to stay clean, a non-slip haft is of great value and could prevent a nasty accident; however, at the butcher's bench, where proper standards of hygiene are being observed, non-slip hafts are not essential. Many amateur butchers like the feel of a wooden haft and, if that is your particular haft of choice, then select knives made of that material. My knives have rubber or resin hafts, simply because the most comfortable knives I have selected over the years happen to have rubber and resin hafts.

The next big question is, what kind of metal should the blade be made of, carbon steel, stainless steel or some other alloy? Personally, I always select stainless steel as I find it easy to sharpen; carbon steel may be the toughest blade material but it is also a devil to sharpen, at least in my experience. I would not touch a carbon steel blade, except perhaps in the field, in a survival setting where you may want to chop down branches with your knife, but at the butcher's bench I would opt for stainless steel every time.

And so we come to the knives themselves, which can be divided neatly into two categories: those used in the field for the work involved in preparing small game for transportation from the field to the butcher's bench, and those used at the bench for the actual butchering.

FIELD BUTCHERING KNIVES

With game birds there is no field dressing required, you simply pick the bird up by the neck and take it home to hang intact. Small game (that is, rabbits and hares) needs to be legged and paunched (both these processes are covered in Chapter 4; if you are not familiar with the terms skip forward and have a quick look at the processes so that you understand the following comments). Legging will occur very shortly after you have killed your quarry; the kind of blade you require to pierce the fairly tough skin between the sinew and tibia of the rabbit's back leg, is one with a very pronounced point that is kept razor sharp. With the point I pierce the skin in the hind leg, at the top of the cavity between the tendon and tibia then, with the centre section of the blade, I make a downward slit. Due to the limited space in this cavity, the centre section of the knife needs to be fairly narrow. Though legging can be carried out with a folding knife, I prefer to use a small sheath knife.

The next process that will have to be carried out in the field is the paunching of the rabbit, which should occur when you get back to your car. This requires making a fine incision in the

A selection of field butchering knives.

The Buck Woodsman is an ideal model for legging.

The Buck caping knife with gutting hook.

rabbit's abdomen that is then enlarged, to allow the intestines to be removed. Because this generally takes place back at the vehicle, the intestines can be placed in a bucket and not thrown away on the farmer's land, which is untidy and unprofessional. Some hunters bury the intestines, however this is a waste if you have ferrets or dogs that have been brought up on a natural diet, as both will happily eat the intestines, with the exception of the stomach. However, the stomach can be slit open and the contents (which are nothing more than digested vegetation) placed on your compost heap; the empty stomach can then be fed to the ferrets or dogs, who will now happily eat them.

The incision in the rabbit's abdomen to facilitate paunching has to be precisely made, not going too deep or you will open the intestine with the tip of the knife and bring the stomach contents into contact with the meat; this is not an irreversible mistake, but it is something that you must try to avoid as, the cleaner the butchering, the better the end product. To make the precise incision required for paunching, the finer the blade and the sharper the point the better. I have found that the knife which best fits this description is a filleting knife, as used by fishermen, or a small skinning knife with a gutting hook, known as a caping knife, such as the one made by Buck for elk skinning.

The caping knife has a very fine point, though not as fine as the point on a filleting knife. The point of the caping knife, however, is still well suited to making fine incisions and, once the incision is made, the blade can be flipped over and the gutting hook placed in the incision. By drawing the knife downwards, the hook then safely opens the abdomen. I say safely, because the back of the hook, which comes into contact with the intestine, is blunt ensuring that the intestines are not pierced; only the portion of

LEFT: A filleting knife is my favoured tool for opening a rabbit's abdomen.

My general purpose field knife, with non-slip haft in bright orange so that it does not get lost in long grass or other vegetation.

the hook which comes into contact with the skin of the abdomen is sharp.

For the beginner the gutting hook provides the safest option. The caping knife is a skinning knife (that is what the term caping means) and,

as with all skinning knives, the Buck caping knife has a wedge-shaped blade. This means that, from the cutting edge to the back of the knife, the blade thickens as with any wedge. The reason for the wedge shape is so that, when the knife is worked between the flesh and the skin of an animal, it forces the two apart – just like a wedge used to split a log in two – making for a very clean separation between the flesh and the pelt, which is most important if you intend to make use of the pelt.

If you decide to use a filleting knife for paunching, then you want the smallest filleting knife that you can find; the blade on mine is just 3¾in (9.5cm) in length, which is perfect. The filleting knife should be kept in the car and reserved solely for the purpose of opening the rabbit's abdomen; use the fine delicate blade of a filleting knife for anything other than cutting into flesh and you will ruin it, by snapping off the all-important pointed blade tip.

The only other knife that is required in the field is a tough, folding pocket-knife to carry out any coarse jobs, so that you are not tempted to use your field butchering knives to do the work. Each knife has its own purpose and it should be kept strictly for that purpose alone. This point cannot be overstressed and is one of the golden rules relating to knife care. The other main rule is to keep the blade sharp at all times: a blunt knife is a useless tool.

KNIVES FOR BUTCHERING

When butchering plucked birds there is very little need for a knife, with just two incisions being required: the first along the underside of the neck to give access to the base of the neck bone so that it can be removed; the second incision being in the vent to allow for the removal of the entrails. Both of these incisions have to be precise, especially the one in the vent, so a small, fine blade is required that is supremely sharp and which offers a fine, easy to manoeuvre point. Both the filleting and the caping knife fit that description and make

A broad-bladed skinning knife, like this Scandinavian knife from Casstrom, covers more ground with each stroke than a thinner blade. Broader blades also have a thicker wedge, so they are more effective at separating the pelt from the flesh.

A cleaver is the preferred implement for cutting through bone.

excellent knives for the butchering of poultry and game birds.

Believe it or not, birds can also be skinned, just like rabbits, a technique that used to be quite common in America but is rarely seen in this country. Skinning a bird can be done in a fraction of the time that it takes to pluck it, so it is a technique well worth learning, especially in these health-conscious times when so many cooks remove the skin of a bird to reduce the fat content. To skin a bird you need a good, broad-bladed skinning knife, with a blade width from cutting edge to back of 1in (2.5cm) and a blade length of 3in (7.5cm).

With the butchering of a rabbit, hare or squirrel there are two distinct tasks to be carried out at the butcher's bench: the first being the skinning of the animal; the second is the actual jointing of the carcase. For skinning you require a knife specifically designed for the task, which, as previously mentioned, will have a wedge-shaped blade to separate the skin from the flesh; despite what some people believe, the blade of the skinning knife should be nice and sharp, so as to cut through the connective tissue joining the skin to the flesh.

Some hunters say that the skinning knife should be blunt, so that you do not cut through the skin, however, this makes the job more difficult and requires the use of more force to complete the task; this in itself is more likely to cause a slip that pierces the valuable pelt. A nice sharp blade will glide smoothly between the flesh and the skin, requiring minimal pressure; if you do not rush the movement, a sharp knife is much less likely to pierce the pelt than a blunt one. The caping knife with its 3½in (9cm) blade length and 1in (2.5cm) blade width is an ideal beginner's skinning knife for small game. As your skill increases, you can progress to a skinning knife with a thicker blade, up to 2in (5cm) in width, which will cover more ground with every stroke than can be covered by the thinner blade. However, it does take more skill to handle the bigger blade which, if allowed to run out of control, will severely nick the pelt, so a broader blade may best be left until you have developed your technique.

The same knife used to skin the rabbit can also be used to joint the carcase – that means to separate it into portions – but do not use it to cut through the bone of the neck, back or legs as you will end up tacking great nicks out of the blade, which will radically reduce its ability to dress the carcase in a presentable fashion. To cut through bone use a cheap, heavy, large-bladed knife or, better still, buy a smaller cleaver, which is the perfect tool for the job.

There are very few knives required at the butcher's bench; having lots of knives will not make you any better at the butchering of animals and birds and, in fact, the more blades you use, the more complex you make the procedure and the more edges you have to keep razor sharp. What you want as a non-professional is a quick and simple process, so keep your knives to a minimum. The key to a knife's success as a butchering tool lies entirely with the sharpness of the edge: blunt, moderately sharp, or even very sharp are not sufficient; the knife used for butchering must have a finely dressed edge that is razor sharp. I have found that most hunters and smallholders do not know how to bring a knife up to such a high level of sharpness, so we will look at the subject for a moment: it is not complicated but there is a knack to it that can be acquired with a bit of perseverance.

Sharpening the Edge of a Blade

The first thing that you need in order to sharpen a blade is a sharpening stone. This can be acquired from any hardware store and does not have to be expensive; in fact the one I use was bought in a pound shop over fifteen years ago and still offers good service today. A sharpening stone has a rough side and a smooth side. The rough side is used when a knife has become blunt and out of shape, the coarse stone removes significant amounts of metal to redress the blade. In all honesty, you should not require the use of this side of the stone, because you should never allow your blades to become blunt: a blunt knife is the product of neglect or ignorance. The smooth side of the stone is used to bring up the sharpness of the edge, removing far less metal than is removed by the rough side.

Some stones can be used dry, while others should have water or oil applied to the stone during use. I prefer an oilstone, which reduces the level of friction when the knife is being sharpened and leaves a smoother finish than a dry stone. There are special honing oils for oilstones but any light oil, such as three-in-one, will serve just as well. If a blade has been really badly abused, or the point has snapped off, then the edge or point can be redeemed by the use of a grind wheel. However, this is best left to somebody who has experience of grind wheels as they can be very aggressive and the knife can be ground down to the size of a toothpick before you realize what has happened.

A small hand-held grinding tool, such as those used by modellers, which takes mini carbide wheels, can also be used to recover an abused blade edge or broken point; they are much less aggressive than a bench grinder and, therefore, much more controllable. The use of a grind wheel may, occasionally, be required for your field knives, but your butchering knives

A coarse sharpening stone and two fine sharpening stones.

should never get into such a poor condition, as their edge should be kept in a constant state of sharpness.

1. To sharpen your knife, your stone should first be secured to the top of a work-bench. Though your knives should never be allowed to become blunt, we will look at the sharpening of a blunt knife, so that you have the necessary knowledge to restore a completely blunt knife with rust on the blade. This knowledge will enable you to purchase second-hand knives and bring them back into service. Second-hand knives are well worth looking at, especially old ones, which can have extremely fine blades and can be purchased very cheaply. Begin by holding the knife by the haft and resting it on the edge of your workbench; then, using a small hand-held grinding tool set at low speed and fitted with a carbide wheel, grind along one side of the blade with the carbide wheel at a 20-degree angle to the edge.

2. If the blade is severely blunt, then several passes the full length of the edge with the carbide wheel may be necessary. The carbide wheel can also be used to restore the point of a blade that has been snapped off, simply by carefully reshaping the blade. The metal that makes up the blade has been hardened by heat treatment and will hold an edge so, if necessary, you can grind back quite deeply into the width of the blade to reshape it and restore the point.

3. Using a light touch, a carbide wheel can also be used to remove rust from the surface of a blade. Rust is the result of the knife being stored in damp conditions or blood, which is very corrosive, being left on the blade.

4. Moving onto the oilstone, lay the blade onto the coarse side of the stone, with the edge resting against the stone and the blade angled at 20 degrees: the angle is very important, too steep and you will blunt the knife edge, too shallow and you

A small and inexpensive grinding tool.

In order to be used safely, a sharpening stone should be secured to the top of a workbench or held in some kind of vice.

will not remove sufficient metal to redress the edge. The widest part of the blade should be covering the stone and the blade should be straight across the stone, not tilted.

A mini carbide wheel.

process should be repeated about ten times. Then begin at the other end of the stone, with the other side of the blade in contact with the stone and draw ten strokes up the stone in the same way as before.

6. It is important that both sides of the blade receive the same number of strokes, as the symmetry of the edge has a direct correlation to its level of sharpness; if one side receives ten strokes and the other twelve, the edge will not be uniform. Working the blade on the coarse side of the stone takes out any deformities in the blade not removed by the carbide wheel and puts it back into the correct shape and symmetry to receive a sharp edge. The purpose of the coarse side of the stone is not to sharpen the edge, that is the role of the smooth side.

7. Now that the blade is the correct shape, place it against the smooth side of the stone (in exactly the same way as you did on the coarse side of the stone) and give it ten strokes down the stone and then ten strokes up. The knife edge will now be sharp: at this point many hunters and smallholders bring the sharpening operation to a halt; however, a sharp knife is simply not good enough for butchering tasks,

5. Now draw the blade down and across the stone, maintaining the angle and keeping the blade straight. Do not force the blade against the stone, but allow it to move lightly across the surface. Once the point has moved across the stone, return to the starting point and repeat the process. The

A rusty blade with a broken tip like this, can be quickly and easily restored by the light use of a carbide wheel.

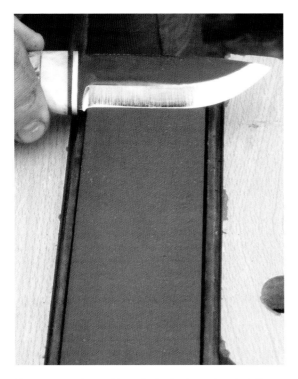

The correct starting position to begin the sharpening of a knife.

Maintaining light pressure, move the blade steadily down the stone, proceeding from the hilt to the point, constantly maintaining the 20-degree angle essential for the establishment of a sharp edge. This process should be repeated about ten to fifteen times, depending on the dullness of the edge.

whether in the field or at the butcher's bench, so the blade has to be made razor sharp and this is done using an implement called a sharpening steel.

8. A sharpening steel, unlike the sharpening stone, removes almost no metal from the edge; the purpose of the steel is to straighten the edge, which takes the sharp knife to a whole new level of razor sharpness. If you have never used a sharpening steel before, you will be amazed at the difference it can make to the level of edge sharpness. No professional butcher would ever consider using a blade that had not first been stroked across a steel and the amateur butcher should make the steel an essential part of their butchery kit.

9. To use a steel: hold the handle in one hand, then place the blade against the steel, just below the handle, in exactly the same way that you placed the blade against the stone, with the blade at the all-important 20-degree angle. Now, draw the blade slowly and lightly down and across the steel, until the point comes away from the steel. Next, place the opposite side of the blade in the same position, in contact with the bottom of the steel and draw up and across the steel until the point comes away from the steel. Repeat the process about ten times for both sides of the blade.

Whilst you are carrying out butchery tasks, the knife blade should be stroked down the sharpening steel every dozen or so cuts, to keep the blade constantly in a razor-sharp state. If the blade is allowed to lose its edge, even slightly, then the quality of the job you are able to perform will diminish and the risk of accidents increases. Whereas a sharp edge glides through flesh, a blunt edge becomes snagged and the amateur who uses more force to get the blade through risks a slip that can prove very painful if a hand gets caught. Therefore, this seems like an ideal moment to take a look at how to use a knife.

An example of a quality sharpening steel. A quality sharpening steel is quite expensive, costing roughly £20, but it will last a lifetime if used correctly.

The knife should be turned over and again set at a 20-degree angle, then drawn up the stone the same number of times that it travelled down the stone.

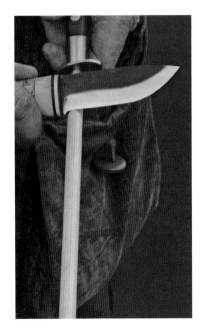

Holding the steel in one hand, place the knife horizontally across the top end of the steel, with the hilt of the knife against the edge of the steel. The all-important 20-degree angle must be established, with the steel in the same position as it is with a sharpening stone.

Now draw the knife steadily down and across the steel, applying a moderate amount of pressure and making sure that you go all the way to the tip of the point. Repeat the process about twelve to fifteen times.

Then turn the knife over and place it at the bottom of the steel, in the same way that you placed it at the top of the steel, then repeat the procedure.

How to Use a Knife

The key to using a knife is never to force it, if a knife refuses to move forward then the reason is simply that the blade is not sufficiently sharp. The very lightest of pressure is all that you should ever apply to a sharp knife, which is sufficient to cut through fur, skin or flesh with the greatest of ease; if this is not the case then return to the sharpening stone and sharpening steel. You can hold a knife in a number of ways: with the blade facing up or down, with the blade side on, or holding it like a scalpel; it all depends on the kind of cut you are going to make.

With the blade facing up or down, the cut is normally a long one, using the point of the blade – when you make an incision into the rabbit's abdomen to remove the paunch, for example. When the blade is side on, you will usually be carrying out a circular cut, such as cutting around the flesh of the rabbit's hind leg before popping the hip joint. When the knife is held like a scalpel, you will be carrying out precision work with the point of the blade – cutting around the vent to access a bird's entrails, for example.

Remember, the knife does not have to stay in one position, but can move about in the hand from one position to another, in order to accommodate the terrain of the carcase. No matter what position you hold the knife in, you should never rest any of your fingers or your thumb on the blade; this is obviously a very dangerous way to hold a knife, all the fingers and the thumb should be on the haft, behind the guard if there is one.

When making a cut, bring the thickest part of the blade possible into contact with the carcase. Some people rely far too heavily on

The cutting edge of the blade facing upwards: a technique used for making long incisions; working away from you and used when opening the abdomen of the rabbit for paunching, for example.

The blade in a downward position: the preferred option for straight and usually deep cuts; used when severing the heads of rabbits or chickens, or for the removal of the front legs of a rabbit.

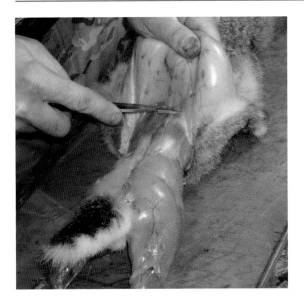

The cutting edge is held side on: used when the knife is being utilized for skinning, or for making circular cuts, when working around the joint in the hind leg of a rabbit, for example.

The knife being held like a scalpel: so that the point is under a high degree of control, a technique utilized for the very delicate work that forms part of the skinning process, and part of the butchery process.

the point; remember, the point is the weakest part of the blade and the further down the blade you go, the stronger it gets. Good knife handling means that you use the thickest (and thus the strongest) part of the knife possible for the given cut. Those who rely on using the point tend to snap it off sooner or later, as the point is only capable of completing fine work and it not designed to be used for heavier cuts.

Use a knife in the correct manner and it will last you a lifetime; however, use the tip all the time and you will soon need to reshape the blade or replace the knife. Blood is a very corrosive substance that can seriously damage metal, so after every butchering session your knives need to be well cleaned. Firstly, wash the knife in warm water with a small amount of detergent added so that all the blood and animal fats are removed. Use a small sponge to wash the knife along the back to avoid cutting yourself.

Once the knife has been thoroughly washed, leave it to dry naturally and then pour vinegar

Make a conscious effort never to rest your fingers or your thumb on the blade.

Butchering knives are extremely sharp and the slightest contact with your hand will produce a deep wound that bleeds heavily, so care must be taken when washing knives. This is the correct way to wash a knife safely.

This is the correct way to safely apply a protective coat of oil to the blade.

over both sides of the blade. Vinegar is a non-abrasive, antiseptic cleanser that will leave the blade deeply clean and hygienic. I do not like to use chemical cleaners, and opt instead for vinegar, which is a natural product that has been used by man for over 7000 years. Again, leave the knife to dry naturally and then apply a very fine coat of oil to the blade, in order to prevent it from rusting – a process that is started when moisture comes into contact with the metal. As with washing, apply the coat of oil with a soft clean rag, working along the back of the knife.

PLUCKING MACHINES

Plucking is a laborious undertaking and one that I try to avoid at all costs; I usually resort to skinning birds but, if the bird is required for roasting, then plucking is the only option. If you have large numbers of birds to do, then it is well worth considering the acquisition of a plucking machine, which will radically speed up the process. A professional can pluck a bird in five minutes but the amateur requires half an hour or more; that's not too bad if you only have to deal with one or two birds a week, but if you are running a small venture from your smallholding, supplying geese or turkeys to the Christmas market, for example, then you will want to pluck at a much faster rate. This is where the plucking machine comes into its' own, as it can dry pluck a bird in roughly five minutes and can be quickly mastered. The plucking machine is basically a rotating drum, powered by an electrical motor, with dozens of rubber fingers on the drum that pluck the feathers as the drum rotates.

MECHANICAL HUMANE DISPATCHERS

Some people just cannot bring themselves to break a bird's neck with their bare hands and there is no shame in that; if you cannot do it then don't try because if you hesitate or panic you will prolong the process, or worse still, cause injury instead of death. If you are unable to kill with your bare hands, then there is an alternative method: the use of a mechanical humane dispatcher. These hand-held or wall-mounted devices work like a pair of pliers; the neck of the bird is simply placed in the jaws of the dispatcher and when it is closed the bird's neck is broken, resulting in death. Humane dispatchers are completely foolproof, as they never fail to dispatch a bird cleanly.

When it comes to large birds like geese and turkeys, and even some of the large cockerels, the neck is simply too big to be broken by hand and so a broom handle is used. The handle is placed across the neck, at the base of the skull and then, standing with a foot on either end of the broom handle, you pull on the bird's body and rotate it forward, breaking the neck. Done properly this method is very quick and humane, although it is also a somewhat brutal method; you have to bend over close to the bird and can therefore see into the bird's eyes, as its neck is broken. If you pull too hard you will also detach the bird's head from its neck, resulting in the release of a lot of blood. The broom handle technique is not suitable for someone who has not killed large birds before and so, under those circumstances, the humane dispatcher is the best option.

CUTTING BOARDS AND BUTCHER'S BLOCKS

Where Should You Butcher?

Although one of the main objectives when butchering is to keep the entire process as clean as possible, the home butcher will be carrying out the entire procedure: from killing, through to skinning or plucking, and then on to the jointing of the meat, so there is going to be some mess involved. Plucking and skinning can be very messy, with feathers flying everywhere, going in your hair, up your nose and sticking to your clothes; so plucking is not something you want to carry out in your nice clean kitchen.

Skinning is less messy, but if doing a number of rabbits there can be a reasonable amount of fine hair flying about. Whether dealing with small game or birds, you are going to have some blood spill, and blood, if not cleaned up immediately, can stain wooden work surfaces. For these reasons I believe the butchering process is best carried out in a small butcher's workshop: this need be nothing more than a six-by-four shed, with a workbench and nails in the centre roof beam, from which small game or birds may be hung.

I do my butchering in a twelve-by-twelve stone barn, where I also keep my guns and ferreting equipment. On a shelf beneath the workbench you will need to keep several buckets: a large one for holding warm water, with roughly 4tsp (20ml) of vinegar in it to keep your work area and hands clean; a small bucket to contain the guts when they are removed, and a second small bucket to hold heads. For feathers you will want a dustbin and, to take the livers, hearts and kidneys, a large plastic bowl and a smaller one for the lungs. You will, of course, keep your knives, a sharpening stone and a sharpening steel in your workshop.

The only remaining items that you will need in your butcher's workshop are several hand towels, some cloths and an apron or dustcoat. In old-fashioned butchers' shops, the floor was liberally sprinkled with shavings to soak up any blood spillages and I think this is a good practice for the home butcher's workshop. Do not forget that game birds and small game will be butchered during the winter months, when the light may be poor, so it is a good idea to have your butcher's workshop equipped with an electric light.

If you carry out butchering operations during the summer months, which is quite feasible as wood pigeon, rabbit, chicken and hare can all be acquired year-round, you will need some kind of meat safe located in a cool place, where the small game or birds may hang until they are butchered. This is essential in order to keep flies off the carcase, which can cover a bird or small game animal in maggot eggs remarkably quickly. I have seen rabbits that, within five minutes of being killed in warm weather, have had maggot eggs all around the eyes, up the nostrils and in the ears, presenting obvious food safety implications.

In warm weather, small game or birds should be placed in a bag of light cotton canvas shaped just like a pillowcase, as soon as they are shot or killed by hand and the bag should then be tied tightly shut with a piece of string. A light cotton canvas is used because it allows airflow and obviously keeps flies off. Do not use bags made of manmade fabrics, as in warm weather they usually cause the kill to sweat, which accelerates the process of decomposition and is the reason why everything goes off more quickly in warm conditions.

The meat safe mentioned above need be nothing more than a wooden cupboard with a mesh door, the kind of mesh used on pantries, which allows for a free flow of air, whilst excluding flies; such mesh is available from good hardware stores. If you can acquire a quantity of old slate tiles you can also line the meat safe with them, by simply nailing them to the sides of the cupboard on the inside. The effect of the tiles will be to make your meat safe much cooler.

chapter two

The Techniques of Humane Dispatch

THE DISPATCHING OF RABBITS

Introduction

(I shall not be dealing with the dispatching of hares because the hare coming to the butcher's bench will have been shot in the field, or possibly hawked, so there is no need for the home butcher to be able to dispatch it.)

I use the word 'dispatch' because this is the accepted terminology, but it still means killing, which, to my mind, is a better way to term it because it doesn't hide the reality of the action. The home butcher must come to terms with the reality: not to salve his or her sensibilities but for the sake of the animal being killed. The home butcher must be clinical and deliberate in order to perform the technique used quickly, cleanly and, above all, correctly, so that no suffering is caused whatsoever; the animal or bird is simply alive one minute and dead the next – having had no inkling of its impending demise.

Firstly, you must study the technique in great depth, until it is absolutely clear in your mind what is required; then you must examine yourself honestly, to find out if you have the required psychology to carry out the task with the required level of detachment. As mentioned above, the home butcher can be either male or female: the dispatching of birds and small game is not a matter of strength, but a matter of technique and so it is a craft that can be performed by both sexes; even children can carry out the butchering of birds or small game if they are correctly trained.

The Neck Chop

Many people will tell you that the only clean way to kill a rabbit is to use the neck break, which refers to the twisting or wringing of the neck until the upper vertebra snaps and the spinal cord is broken, detaching the body from the brain and causing death. The neck break is, however, a technique that requires quite a lot of skill: the rabbit's head must be cupped in one hand between fingers and thumb and rotated in one direction, whilst the body is rotated in the other; then, at the right moment, there is a backward tilt of the head, the rotation and tilt causing the spinal damage.

Get this technique wrong and it will put you off killing rabbits for life; you will inflict a terrible injury without causing death and you could even paralyse the rabbit rather than killing it. Leave this technique to those who are experienced in it; if you must learn it then do so under the tuition of someone who is an expert at the neck break, like a ferreter. As a ferreter I sometimes use this technique and can report that when the neck breaks you can actually feel the break occur through the hand cupping the neck, which quite a number of people would find off-putting.

I have read numerous books that outline the use of the neck break without explaining the difficulties involved, which, in my opinion, is irresponsible. The neck break is a highly skilled operation that cannot be learnt from the pages of a book. It is also worth noting that this method can result in a painful injury to the thumb known as 'gamekeeper's thumb', which is a tear of the thumb ligament, giving you another very good reason to stay well away from this technique. I shall not mention the neck break again and only brought it up to make you aware of the difficulties this technique offers to the beginner.

The method I advocate for the killing of rabbits – whether they are wild rabbits, bolted by a ferret into a net, or home-reared meat rabbits – is the neck chop. This is a powerful blow, delivered to the base of the skull, which causes major trauma and death through massive internal haemorrhaging. The initial blow instantly renders the rabbit unconscious and death (the point at which the heart stops beating), occurs roughly thirty seconds after the blow has been struck. This technique is extremely humane as the rabbit is rendered unconscious immediately and thus suffers no pain as death occurs.

In an abattoir, cattle, sheep and pigs are slaughtered by first stunning the animal, rendering it unconscious, then slitting its throat with a very sharp knife, causing it to bleed out and the heart to stop. This method is considered the most humane form of dispatch; a claim backed by scientific research with the technique being accepted and accredited by many animal welfare groups.

The neck chop used to kill a rabbit, works on exactly the same principle as the stun and slit method used in abattoirs, except there is no need to cut the throat as the bleeding occurs internally in the neck area. The neck chop is therefore a method of rabbit killing that is easy to learn and very humane. Another great advantage of this technique is that, if you do not deliver the required amount of force to kill the rabbit, you will not cause an agonizing injury – you will simply knock the rabbit out. I have seen this happen several times while

out ferreting: a blow delivered with insufficient force or slightly outside the desired area and the rabbit is knocked out cold, seemingly dead. Then, when placed on the ground, as the ferreter attends to his ferrets, the rabbit suddenly regains consciousness, springs to its feet and runs off at full speed, no worse for its experience. Therefore, the beginner who makes a mistake delivering this technique will not cause the rabbit undue suffering, which should give them the confidence required to make the blow.

Some people are critical of the neck chop and claim that it causes severe bruising to the meat, which is totally misleading. The chop undoubtedly causes a huge amount of bruising, for obvious reasons, but the site of the bruising is the neck where it attaches to the skull. There is no more meat in this area than would fill a teaspoon so, if anyone tells you that the neck chop causes bruising to the rabbit meat, ignore them. The area in which the bruising occurs and where the blood pools is, in fact, cut away in order to remove the head of the rabbit; the damage therefore only occurs in an area that does not even proceed to the butchering process.

Now that you are familiar with my reasoning for teaching the neck chop, let us get down to the actual technique of the procedure. Firstly, take hold of the rabbit by the loins in your left hand (for a right-handed individual) and in the right hand (for a left-handed individual).

If the rabbit has been driven into a net by a ferret, then you do not need to remove the net before delivering the blow. Some books instruct you to take the rabbit by the hind legs, rather than the loins, which will cause stress to the rabbit and make the task more difficult for you. Most rabbits, when taken by the hind legs, jerk powerfully back and forth like a piston, in an attempt to free themselves, in doing so they suffer mental and physical stress. If the rabbit is a big buck the jerks can be very dynamic, making the animal very difficult to control. These jerks can occur just as you are about to land your blow, meaning that you will strike

The thumb locks on here

When you go to pick up a rabbit (unless it is very tame), it will bunch up. Grasp it quickly either side of the spine on the loins

The fingers lock on the opposite side in exactly the same location as the thumb

To deliver a neck chop to a rabbit, it must first be held firmly by the loins.

outside the intended area, or you will miss the rabbit altogether, prolonging a process that, in order to be humane, has to be carried out in seconds.

If a rabbit is taken around the loins with a firm grip, it becomes limp and does not move at all. I believe (although I do not have proof) that the reason for adopting such a posture is that a rabbit held around the loins cannot physically do anything to escape; to struggle is useless, so the rabbit plays possum in the hope that it will be taken for dead and thus the predator may drop its guard, allowing the rabbit a tiny chance to escape.

Place the rabbit across your right leg (for right-handed people) and left leg (for left-handed people) placing the rabbit's ribcage in full contact with the leg, just above the knee. The reason for this is because, if you did not hold the rabbit against yourself to deliver the blow, the rabbit held by the loins can pendulum slightly away from the blow, dissipating the energy of the blow to a sufficient degree that death is not inflicted. To prevent any pendulum movement, the rabbit is placed

against the leg and thus the full force of the blow is transmitted from the side of the hand, in a concentrated manner, into the neck area of the rabbit, delivering a massive degree of physical shock and causing irreversible trauma. With the rabbit in the correct position, place the right hand (for right-handed individuals) and the left hand (for left-handed individuals) roughly 1ft (30cm) away from the rabbit's head and about 4in (10cm) above its body, with the fleshy side of the hand directly behind the head.

In America they use a club to deliver the blow, rather than the side of the hand, which to my mind is massive overkill – a bit like striking a Brazil nut with a sledgehammer – and is not something that I would consider but, if you prefer to use a small wooden or metal club, the option is open to you. One word of warning though, a club makes a sickening thud when it strikes, for the simple reason that the club, being a hard object, is striking a soft object, the rabbit's head, and not everyone can stomach the noise. The chop with the side of the hand makes no such noise.

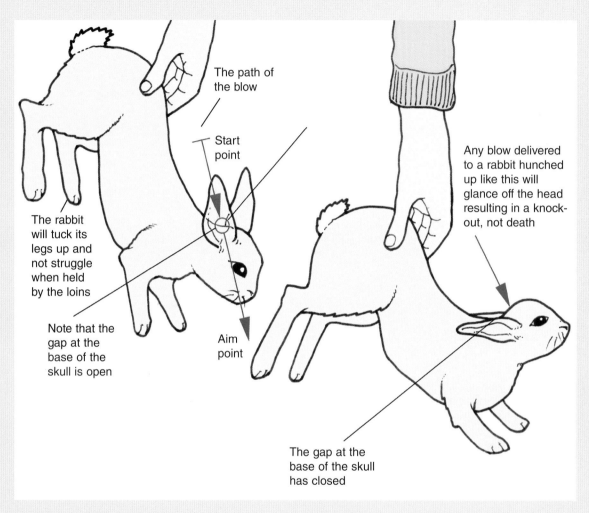

The path of
the blow

Start
point

The rabbit
will tuck its
legs up and
not struggle
when held
by the loins

Note that the
gap at the
base of the
skull is open

Aim
point

Any blow delivered
to a rabbit hunched
up like this will
glance off the head
resulting in a knock-
out, not death

The gap at the
base of the skull
has closed

The body of the rabbit is placed across the upper portion of your leg, the rabbit's ribcage in contact with the leg. If the rabbit is bunched up, with the head raised, a blow delivered in this position will strike the top of the skull and, at best, will only stun the rabbit. To rectify this problem tilt the rabbit forward, pivoting on the ribcage, until the head is down and the blow can go in over the shoulders, to the base of the skull for a fatal effect. Right-handed person: hold loins with left hand and strike with right. Left-handed person: hold loins with right hand and strike with left. If the rabbit bunches its head and neck do not panic or strike; delay the blow momentarily. Tilt the rabbit forward slightly causing the gap to open, at which point you can deliver the blow.

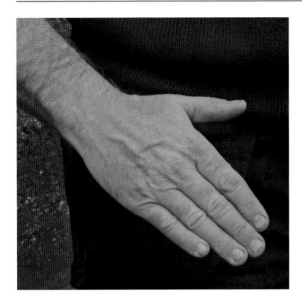

To deliver the blow the hand must be tensed and the fingers pressed together, the thumb being raised.

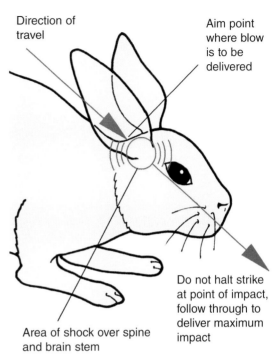

Direction of travel

Aim point where blow is to be delivered

Area of shock over spine and brain stem

Do not halt strike at point of impact, follow through to deliver maximum impact

The starting point for the blow is just behind the rabbit's shoulders, with a trajectory very slightly downward, but mostly forward, so as to enter the dip slightly in front of the shoulders, taking the travel of the blow along the neck and straight into the base of the skull.

If you feel that your hand is not sufficiently strong to deliver the neck chop (perhaps due to a hand injury or deformity) then you can use a club such as this one, which was simply cut from a length of heavy metal tubing. However, be careful if you are using a club; it is possible to smash the rabbit's head to pieces, causing huge internal damage and presenting butchering problems.

To deliver the blow, push all the fingers firmly together and have the thumb raised.

Then move the hand back slightly and with one swift, determined movement strike the rabbit at the base of the skull, sending the blow under the rabbit's ears, the direction of travel for the blow being forward toward the rabbit's nose. Contrary to what most people think, the blow is not delivered to the back of the neck, travelling downward in the direction of the throat. The forward travel of the blow is used to transmit the shock of the blow into the brain area and into the region where the blood and nerve supply, running along the spine, enters the brain; severe impact damage to this area will obviously cause a fatal degree of trauma.

If you make your strike to the back of the neck, rather than the base of the skull, you will be striking an area covered by well developed muscle, which is quite an effective protective layer; there is no major blood vessel running down the back of the neck, so the likelihood of delivering a blow that results in fatal trauma is not very high. You don't even stand a very high chance of breaking the rabbit's neck with a such a blow because, when you strike the back of the neck it will move forward, thus dissipating some of the energy in the strike. Whereas, when the blow is delivered to the base of the skull with forward momentum, the head does not move forward, for the simple reason that heads have no facility to move forward, they can only go from side to side and up and down. So, when a blow is delivered to the base of the skull, the complete lack of forward movement means that the full force of the blow is transmitted to the target area with fatal consequences.

You do not have to make the blow with every ounce of strength that you can muster – a good strong blow is sufficient to do the job – and do not terminate the strike at the point of impact. A karate practitioner, when striking a piece of wood, is not aiming his blow at the piece of wood but at an area below it. If the blow is aimed at the wood, the force of the blow ends when the strike is made, but when aiming at a point below the wood, the energy continues as if the wood is simply an obstruction in the way of the hand's final destination. Your blow to the base of the rabbit's skull must be delivered in the same manner, aiming at a point beyond the intended target area, thus retaining the energy at the point of impact.

I have covered the technique of the neck chop in great detail and given you a lot to think about; however, to give you some perspective, all the information above describes an action that takes, roughly, five to ten seconds to perform. If you are uncertain as to the effect of the first blow, then it is quite acceptable to make a second strike. Even if the first strike is too light to have caused death, it will certainly have rendered the rabbit unconscious; you are therefore not causing any suffering to the rabbit if you deliver a second blow as an insurance policy. I have killed countless numbers of rabbits with the neck chop and can testify to the fact that this method is clean, swift and causes no suffering whatsoever. Just one final point about the neck chop: you may find that you bruise the side of your hand slightly making the strike, but there is not a lot you can do about that.

Muscular Spasms

When you deliver a fatal blow to the base of the rabbit's skull, the rabbit will not go limp immediately. As death occurs, and for approximately thirty seconds after death, the rabbit will produce violent muscular spasms exhibited in the kicking of the back legs. This is normal, the rabbit is not suffering and it does not mean that you have made a mess of the chop; it is simply the body shutting down. This twitching occurs with all small game and birds, whether killed by hand or shot, but it is something that you must be fully prepared for; it is quite common for people new to the killing of animals to think that the muscular spasms are evidence that the animal is still alive, at which point they panic and start to dispatch it all over again, in an attempt to end the perceived suffering.

Twitching is natural so be prepared for it; the degree of twitching varies from one rabbit to the next but generally: the younger the rabbit, the greater the twitch, though the greatest degree of movement is usually seen in the really big, powerful buck rabbits. If you wish to check a rabbit for evidence that death has occurred, then you can tap with your finger in front of an eye: if there is no blink reflex you know the rabbit is dead, but if it blinks it is obviously still alive.

Peeing The Rabbit

When the rabbit is dead, the loss of muscle control in the dead body means that the bladder is relaxed and the contents can leak out so, as soon as the rabbit is dead, the bladder has to be emptied, a process known among ferreters as 'peeing'. Simply hold the rabbit around the ribcage with one hand, with the hind legs facing the ground and apart. Then place the thumb of the other hand on the rabbit's mid-line, about two inches below the ribcage, with the fingers of that hand cupped around the side of the rabbit. Now push inwards with the thumb in the direction of the spine, applying a moderate level of pressure, and then move the thumb down the mid-line towards the hind legs. As you progress down the mid-line you will suddenly see a jet of urine being expelled from the rabbit, in a downward direction from a female rabbit and in a forward direction from a male rabbit. Repeat the process until urine stops being expelled.

The hare, just like the rabbit, must be peed straight after death and likewise the squirrel, if you are inclined to butcher squirrels (and a small number of people in this country do eat them).

HANGING

It is not always possible to butcher your rabbits straight away; if I have been in the field ferreting I frequently do not return until late afternoon, at which point the stock on my smallholding needs tending, and so the rabbits have to wait until the next day to be butchered. This is perfectly acceptable if the rabbits are correctly hung, but a rabbit cannot hang with its intestine still in place, as the bacterial action of the gut continues after death and can taint, or even ruin, the meat. If the intestine is left in the hanging rabbit overnight, the gas build up within it leads to the organ swelling, sometimes to such a degree that the abdomen itself is hugely distended. When you make an incision in the abdomen to remove the guts the swollen intestine, which will be pressing against the abdomen wall, will be pierced, no matter how carefully you make your incision, allowing the contents, which will now be fluid, to escape.

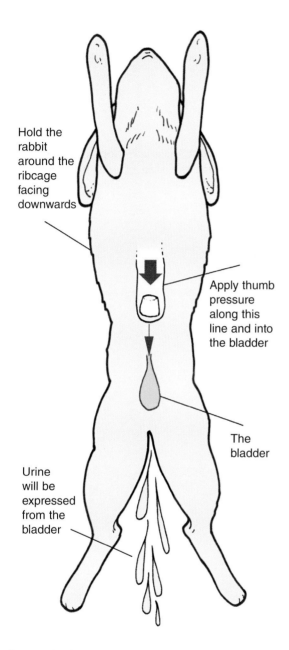

Hold the rabbit around the ribcage facing downwards

Apply thumb pressure along this line and into the bladder

The bladder

Urine will be expressed from the bladder

Run your thumb down the central line of the rabbit's abdomen and you will express the urine from its balder; a process referred to as 'peeing the rabbit'.

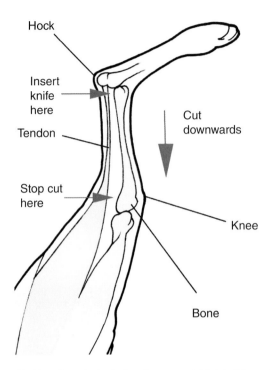

Hock

Insert
knife
here

Tendon

Stop cut
here

Cut
downwards

Knee

Bone

Between the tendon and bone of the hind leg, above the hock, there is a gap and it is into this gap that the incision is made for the legging of a rabbit or hare.

These intestinal contents can foul the pelt or taint the meat, not to mention the mess they will make of your workspace. The removal of the intestine is a process called 'paunching' and, if the rabbits you are butchering are wild, this process may already have taken place in the field. However, if your rabbits are of the meat variety, reared on your holding, then the paunching will take place in your butcher's workshop. Whichever is the case, the process is exactly the same and we shall be covering it in Chapter 4. In order to hang a rabbit you need to carry out a process known as 'legging', which involves making an incision in the gap between the bone and tendon of the hind leg, located above the hock.

To make the incision you will require a knife with a thin blade and a sharp point. Take the rabbit by the leg and drive the tip of the blade through the gap, making your entry just below the hock. When the knife is all the way through, cut down as far as you can, stopping about ¼in (6mm) short of the flesh portion of the hind leg. Now take the foot of the other leg and thread it through the incision you have made (just like threading a length of cotton through the eye of a needle). Keep pushing on the leg until the hock joint goes through the incision, at which point pull back slightly on the leg and you will find that the hock joint locks against the incision, preventing the leg coming back through. You have now legged the rabbit and can hang it up on a 4in (10cm) nail hammered into a beam or similar object. The rabbit should not be hung up with one side against a wall; it must be suspended by the legs and hung openly, so that air can circulate freely on all sides.

Hold the rabbit by the foot of the leg into which you intend to make the incision. Place your knife on the gap between the tendon and the bone, just below the hock, and push the knife point through, with the cutting edge facing downward; make a cut down to a point just short of the leg meat.

Take the rabbit's other foot and thread the end of that foot through the incision you have just made (just like threading cotton through the eye of a needle). Squeeze the rabbit's toes together or they will splay out as you try and thread the foot through the incision, making it impossible to get the foot through.

Once the end of the foot is through the incision pull on it until the hock also comes through the incision; then pull back on the leg and the hock will lock against the incision.

Now the rabbit or hare can be hung.

The legging process outlined above is exactly the same in the case of a hare; the only difference between a hare and a rabbit is that the hare is hung with its paunch (stomach and intestines) left in place and is left to hang for up to fourteen days, in order to intensify the flavour. Fourteen days is the absolute maximum hanging time for a hare; Mrs Beeton, who was an expert game cook, stated that a hare should be well hung for seven to eight days and I would endorse this advice. Though you should not exceed the seven to eight days, there is no absolute necessity to hang for that long as your palate may prefer a milder flavoured, less gamey meat; experiment with different hanging times and remember, the longer a hare hangs, the stronger the flavour becomes.

Hares need to be hung in a cool, dry, dark place, the ideal being an old larder, although very few houses these days still have them. Never hang a rabbit in this way, however, as a rabbit hung for seven to eight days will be reduced to nothing more than a stinking carcase, unfit even for dog meat. However, some people are now hanging paunched rabbit for two or three days and say that this increases the flavour of the meat. This practice is perfectly acceptable and my experiments have shown that the hanging of rabbits does, in fact, increase the intensity of taste; I now routinely hang all my rabbits paunched for at least a day and preferably two.

This practice does, however, make the skinning of the rabbit slightly more difficult, as the cooler the rabbit becomes, the more difficult it is to separate the skin from the underlying flesh. I can skin a rabbit that is still warm in just under five minutes, whereas a rabbit that has been hanging takes me about eight minutes. Hanging small game is not, however, a universal practice; in America for example, they don't even hang hare, let alone rabbit. Many American hunters stipulate that the sooner small game is butchered and cooked the better the flavour. Some of them even butcher their small game as soon as it is shot, right there in the field, jointing the animal

and placing it in a plastic bag and then into a backpack.

So you have a choice: to hang or not to hang? It is entirely up to you and your final decision should not be based on what other people do, but on what produces meat that best suits you palate. To discover what suits you best, simply experiment with different hanging times, starting with no hanging time at all, going up as far as three days for rabbits and eight or nine days for hares. In hot weather, three hours will see your small game turn into a flyblown, stinking mess that is not safe to eat, unless you have a seriously cool place to hang it; instant butchering is therefore the most hygienic approach during a hot summer.

During hot weather I have seen a rabbit, less than an hour after hanging, with fly eggs up its nostrils, in its ears, around its eyes and in the cavity from which the paunch has been removed. The flesh of the rabbit becomes warm and slimy, instead of cool and taut and, as such, is not going to be fit for human consumption. Hanging in warm weather should therefore be confined to those who have a cellar or a specially made cool room; everyone else should butcher the carcase straight away.

Before leaving the subject of hanging, I should like to mention the gut shot rabbit or hare: by this I mean a rabbit or hare that has been shot in the abdomen with a rifle or a shotgun. Either of these weapons, delivering a projectile to the abdominal area of a rabbit or hare, is going to blow the paunch wide open, completely contaminating the abdominal cavity. Small game shot in this way should not be hung, as the contents of the intestine and stomach, which have been violently released all over the abdominal cavity, will decompose into the flesh during the hanging process. Rabbits and hares that have been gut shot can have the front and hind legs removed for meat; the remainder of the carcase can then be used for dog food (if your dog has been raised on a raw meat diet), alternatively the carcase can be used for ferret food.

In fact, the correct place to shoot a rabbit or hare with a rifle is in the head, as this conserves the entire body intact for use as meat. With a shotgun, the target should be the head and upper chest area, thus preserving intact the largest meat-bearing part of the rabbit or hare: the hind legs and loins. Rabbits or hares correctly targeted are safe to hang. Game birds require hanging and some people believe that poultry is improved by a short period of hanging; we will therefore look at the hanging of birds in Chapter 5.

THE DISPATCHING OF BIRDS

All the game birds that you deal with will have been shot, so there is no dispatching involved; however, when it comes to hens, ducks, guinea fowl and quail, which have been raised on the holding, you will have to carry out the dispatching by hand. This is done by breaking the bird's neck, thus severing the spinal cord, cutting off the brain from the body and causing instant death.

Most books and professionals will tell you that a bird must be starved for between twenty-four and thirty-six hours prior to being killed, but this is not a practice that I follow as I believe it to be cruel. The reasoning behind the starvation is to ensure that the digestive tract is empty, thus making it easier to remove the croup and entrails; however, it is quite possible to remove both cleanly, even if the bird has been feeding heavily right up to the very point of death, it just requires a little extra care. Starving birds produces both confusion and stress because it breaks the bird's normal routine; numerous studies with cattle have shown that the presence of stress reduces both the quality and the flavour of the meat.

The other reason that birds are starved is because the abdomen supposedly turns green shortly after death, due to the decomposition of food in the intestine. I have seen birds that did not have their entrails removed until several days after slaughter and observed no evidence

of a greening in the abdomen. Normally a bird would have been plucked and the entrails drawn within a much shorter timeframe, sufficient to prevent any greening of the abdomen, so again, I do not see this as a valid reason for starving birds.

As home butchers, one of the key objectives is to ensure that the animals and birds slaughtered are dispatched with the greatest degree of humane treatment possible. To my mind, a long period of starvation prior to slaughter is tantamount to torture; it is therefore not a practice that we as home butchers should be willing to institute. Many books will state that the starvation is essential, but I know from my own experiences that it most certainly is not.

So let us move on to the actual dispatching of the bird. Commercially produced birds are first stunned by an electric current and then have their throats cut with a sharp knife. The purpose of the stun is to ensure that the bird does not feel the knife cutting its throat, while the throat cut is to sever a major artery, causing the bird to bleed to death. Welfare organizations are very critical of this method, claiming that the level of current required to stun a bird sufficiently not only renders it unconscious, but also shatters numerous bones in the bird's body, leading to bone splinters – an obvious problem for the table bird.

To prevent bone splinters the current is reduced, however, welfare organizations also believe that the birds are then not sufficiently stunned and can feel the knife cutting their throat. Personally I am not convinced that a powerful electric shock, even if the right current is used, is a kind and gentle way to render a bird unconscious. I have only ever been electrocuted by electrified stock-proof fencing, which had a tiny trickle of charge going through it, and it was a horrible sensation. The huge, nineteen-stone pigs that the fence was enclosing would, upon touching the fence, squeal and leap back. I personally cannot see how an electric stun is somehow kind and painless; I think you should just get on with the job and kill the bird outright.

This is not really relevant to the home butcher because you will not be going to the expense of buying stunning equipment, but I mention it to show that the home butcher with his or her unsophisticated set-up can, in actual fact, carry out a more humane operation. Before you get too worried about cutting a bird's throat let me also state that it is not necessary to do it; a bird does not have to have every drop of blood drained from its body to be fit for the table.

Just as a side note, in some countries birds are killed by having their heads placed on a wooden block and then cut clean off in one go, using a very sharp, heavy cleaver. This method may sound brutal but it is a very easy method to master: it is very quick and surprisingly humane as the bird is dispatched instantly; however, this method is also very messy due to the arterial spray from the severed arteries. Despite the ease and efficiency of this method it is a bit too primeval for most people's tastes, so we shall move swiftly on to the dislocation method. This method entails the bird's neck being broken, severing the spinal cord and rupturing the main artery in the neck, bringing about near instantaneous death.

This method of dispatch both renders the bird fully unconscious and bleeds it as well, the blood pooling in the base of the neck behind the skull, at the site of the dislocation. This is the method that was used in slaughterhouses in the past and is, to my mind, far more humane than all the messing around with electric stunning that takes place today.

1. To carry out this method of dispatch first take the bird by the shanks (the leg below the hock). To do this, first hold the bird under your arm as normal, then support it under the chest with the other hand; next move the hand of the arm that is cradling the bird along the belly and down the legs, until you are grasping both shanks. Lower the bird, still supporting the chest, until it is across your thigh, at which point the hand supporting the chest moves round and takes the bird by the neck.

2. You take the neck from behind, at the top end where it meets the head. Most people take the neck between the first and second finger, cupping the second and third fingers under the bird's cheeks and lower beak. I find this uncomfortable, preferring to take the neck between my thumb and first finger, with my first second and third fingers cupped under the bird's cheeks and lower beak. You can experiment for yourself with both holds, to see which best suits you: take a tame chicken and place it in the dispatch position, which will do it no harm as long as you do not pull on the neck.

3. A lot of people think that it is cruel to hold a bird by the shanks, but it does the bird no harm whatsoever, neither damaging the bone structure nor the supporting tissue. When a bird is held by the shanks in an upside-down position you also do not need to worry that its wings will flap about madly as, in this position, birds behave as if sedated. In my experience, not even very nervous or highly aggressive birds make the slightest effort to struggle when held in this manner, so there is no need for restraints like tying down the bird's wings with a length of string. When you become experienced in this method of dispatch the bird will not be held in the upside-down position, by the shanks, for more than between thirty to fifty seconds.

4. With your grip fully established on the bird's neck, extend it to its natural full length by moving the hand in a downward direction; when this point is reached make a strong downward thrust, combined with a backward twist of the neck. These two movements must be performed as one flowing action, with no hesitation as this will cause undue suffering to the bird. The part that concerns most people is the back twist, but it is simply a matter of rotating the wrist at the end of the downward thrust, in order to cause a dislocation between the skull and the first vertebra of the bird's neck. The important point to

ABOVE: The dispatching of a bird begins by holding the bird under your arm as normal.

RIGHT: Then support the bird's chest with the other hand, at the same time moving the hand of the arm cradling the bird swiftly and gently down to take the bird by the shanks (the area of leg between the hock and the foot). When held by the shanks birds do not struggle, as demonstrated by this duck.

Lower the bird across your upper leg, still supporting the chest.

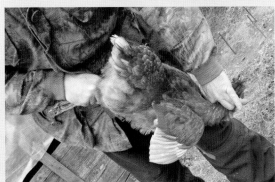

Swiftly move the hand supporting the chest around to take the bird's neck, close to the base of the skull, with the neck firmly held between the first finger and thumb.

It is the right hand that is in position around the neck, with the fingers cupped under the bird's cheeks and lower beak.

Extend the bird's neck to its full length, and then make a further strong downward pull, followed by a backward twist to dislocate the bird's neck.

The broomstick method of dispatch.

remember is to continue to apply forward pressure as the back twist occurs, which should be achieved as the wrist rotates the hand backwards, the forward pressure coming from the fork created around the bird's neck by the web between the thumb and the first finger.

5. Now to address the question of how much pressure should be applied to the neck in order to effect a clean dislocation. It must be remembered that the actual mechanics of the movement, if properly performed, are responsible for the dislocation far more than the physical force applied, so technique is more important than brute strength. The amount of force involved is relatively small and, if too much force is applied, the head can be pulled clean off the neck leaving you with a bloody neck stump and blood spitting out from the neck. The neck stump has a tendency to move about for a short while which is somewhat macabre. But the worst thing about pulling the bird's head off is that the blood soaks the feathers and since blood is not merely wet, but also very sticky, the plucking of the bird becomes a very tedious and messy task, with the blood-stained feathers sticking to your hands.

6. When the neck is dislocated the bird's wings will begin to flap about with fury; do not worry, this does not mean that you have failed to kill the bird, on the contrary, the flapping begins the moment a fatal dislocation occurs and is a sign that you have done the job properly. The flapping is the same action as the twitching referred to earlier under the section on rabbit dispatch; the flapping indicates the life ebbing from the bird's body. Be prepared for this, do not panic and do not drop the bird in surprise; I have seen birds with a fully dislocated neck when let go, run off for a short distance or fly up in the air to waist height. I once saw a bird that had received a fatal shot to the head fly one hundred yards after being shot, before

dropping to the floor. This physical movement after death is not evidence of life and it does not mean that the bird is suffering, it is simply the body shutting down: because the brain has been disconnected by the dislocation of the neck, there is no facility for the bird to feel any pain or distress.

The more vigorous and healthy the bird, the greater the amount of flapping; sick and very elderly birds offer no more than a few flaps of the wings. This is a point well worth noting: if a bird you have dispatched offers only a few flaps of the wings with little fury, you must question the health of that bird and thus question the safety of the meat for table use. Part of being a butcher is being able to recognize the signs of ill health in a bird or animal, so that you do not prepare meat that could be hazardous to human health, but more about this subject later.

7. If you think you have not killed the bird, there is an easy way to check: simply feel with your finger and thumb at the base of the skull. If the bird is still alive you will clearly be able to feel the skull, still attached to the vertebrae of the neck; if there is a gap between the base of the skull and the vertebrae into which your finger fits, you know that the dislocation is complete and the bird is dead. Do not judge the presence of life in the bird by looking at its eye, as the eye of a bird will blink for a short while after death has occurred.

The flapping referred to above, occurs with such a degree of violence that the meat on the wings can be damaged if the wings bash against something like a wall, so make sure that there is plenty of space all around you when you dispatch a bird. Do not be tempted to hold the bird's wings down until the flapping reflex has passed; the reflex is very powerful and takes quite a bit of restraint and, even if you do manage to fully restrain the wings, the reflex will merely occur in the legs instead, which you have let go of in order to restrain the wings. Just keep hold of the shanks after you have dispatched the bird and, after a few minutes, the flapping will have subsided.

8. In the past, professional chicken dispatchers would have a number of metal cones, just like upturned traffic cones, attached to a frame and they would place the dispatched bird into a cone, which contained the bird whilst restraining the wings, allowing the twitching to pass without any damage occurring to the meat on the bird's wings. If you can get your hands on a traffic cone, you could upturn it and attach it to a frame and use it in the same way that the old professionals used their cones.

An old-fashioned cone hanger used historically in the poultry industry to prevent birds from fluttering after dispatch. Try to fashion something of this nature for your own use.

If you are dispatching more than one bird I consider it important not to allow the other birds to see you dispatch one of their number; birds are not overly intelligent and probably do not have the capacity to figure out that they are next in line but, in case I am wrong, I never dispatch one bird in front of another. When dispatching small birds like quail and pigeon, use the method already described, but reduce the amount of pressure you apply to the neck radically or you will pull the bird's head, which is very small and fragile, clean off its neck.

The neck dislocation outlined above is an effective method of dispatch for normal sized birds but, if the bird is a large cockerel or one of the very large meat birds, then the neck is too big to be manipulated by the above method. Geese and turkeys, due to their size, cannot be dispatched using the above method. For these larger birds I would recommend the use of a mechanical device: a hand-held or wall-mounted dispatching device.

To use a hand-held dispatching device, simply place the bird's neck in the jaws of the dispatcher and squeeze. The neck is instantly broken and the job is done. The hand-held dispatcher will deal with birds up to 14lb (6kg). For bigger birds you require a wall-mounted dispatcher, which

is a simple device to use: you simply place the neck of the bird in the U-shaped gap and pull the lever down smartly. This device will break the neck of the bird and sever the spinal cord and form a cavity into which the blood will drain when the bird is hung. This device is not intended to sever the bird's head, so a regulating screw is

Pigeons and other small birds have very small necks and, if you pull on them too hard, the head will come clean off in your hand.

RIGHT: The hand-held dispatcher.

FAR RIGHT: The wall-mounted dispatcher.

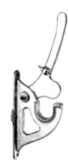

used to adjust the gap to facilitate the size of the bird you are killing.

Ducks can be dispatched using the neck dislocation as described above, but they generally have a stronger neck than a hen and some people have a problem dislocating it. I personally use the broom handle method for killing a duck, which means placing a broom handle across the duck's neck, then standing on either end of the broom handle, pulling the bird up and forward suddenly to effect a dislocation. Performed quickly and correctly this method is very effective and humane; however, if you have not been well tutored in this method you can make a real mess of it, so it should not be attempted unless you have received instruction from someone who can perform it skilfully.

If you do not feel confident killing ducks using the neck dislocation method, then dispatch them in the same manner as larger birds with the aid of a humane dispatcher. If you are experienced with the use of air rifles, you could use an air rifle with a full 12ftlb power output in .22 or .25 calibre, delivering the shot at point-blank range into the bird's brain, which is located just behind the eye. Shooting will only work with tame birds that you are able to get close to. Under no circumstances should you

have a person hold the bird you wish to shoot, as this is a recipe for disaster; the slightest misalignment of the barrel or a nudge of the barrel at the point of discharge and the person holding the bird could be seriously injured. Therefore, experienced air gun handlers, who know exactly what they are doing, should only ever carry out shooting.

Some books suggest the use of the air rifle as the easiest way to kill a bird, but that is not the case as using an air rifle, even at point-blank range, requires a high degree of skill. In fact, the use of an air rifle at extremely close quarters, usually in an enclosed space, is one of the most dangerous applications of a rifle; it requires a thorough understanding of how a pellet will behave when it strikes the target. For example, if a shot is taken from the side into a bird's head, which is fairly narrow, the pellet, especially if it is a hunting pellet designed to penetrate, may enter one side and exit the other and then ricochet; ricochets, due to their unpredictable nature, are always dangerous and can cause injury. So, if you are not experienced with an air rifle, then do not even consider using one to dispatch a bird or you may end up doing yourself more harm than the bird you are trying to kill.

chapter three

The Importance of Meat Inspection and Hygiene

MEAT INSPECTION

If you intend to become a home butcher, one of the skills that you need to possess, in order to produce safe meat, is the ability to recognize disease in birds and small game. The reason for this is simple: diseased animals can cause illness in human beings. This is not always the case, however: a rabbit with myxomatosis, for example, can be eaten without causing illness, although I would not advise such a course of action unless you are in a desperate survival situation.

As a rule, you should reject every bird or animal that comes to your butcher's bench if it presents signs of disease. Some diseases carried by animals will only induce mild symptoms, but others, for example, bird flu, can kill the person consuming the meat. Four excellent indicators of a bird or animal's health are: the eye, the nose, the coat or plumage, and the weight. The eye, even in a dead animal or bird, should be bright and there should be no discharge or swelling around it.

The nose, or in the case of a bird the beak, should be free from discharge, and the coat

Note that the eyes of these dead rabbits are clear, bright and healthy.

Fur or feather should have a natural lustre: if this is not present disease should be suspected.

or plumage should be clean, shiny and intact. If there are numerous bald patches, or the feather or fur has lost its natural lustre, you have to wonder if this is not the first sign of disease within the body.

Weight is also a good indicator of a bird or animal's overall condition, so feel the breastbone of a bird and, if it feels skeletal, it is either very old or ill. With small game, weight is carried on the loins and you should not be able to see the ribs through the coat; if you can see the animal's ribs through its coat it is definitely ill. When butchering your own stock, you have the added advantage of being able to observe the bird or rabbit on a daily basis and will soon become aware of ill health. When butchering your own stock you should give the bird or rabbit a quick check over before killing it, for the simple reason that if it is slightly ill it should not be killed, but left to recover and then slaughtered another day.

You should also check the back end of birds and small game for signs of diarrhoea: if it is present then the bird or animal is not fit for consumption. You should also part the coat of small game and the plumage of birds in numerous places across the animal or bird's body; if there is a heavy infestation of parasites, strange markings or discoloration of the skin, then the small game or bird under examination should be rejected.

So far we have looked at the external surface of the animal or bird for evidence of ill health, but we also need to examine the animal or bird internally when carrying out the butchering process. As a home butcher you need to know what the internal anatomy of both small game and birds looks like, clearly understanding the location of all the major organs. This understanding will enable you to tell at a glance if there is something inside the bird or animal that should not be there, a tumour for example; it goes without saying that you do not want to eat anything that has a tumour. So look for any masses within the animal or bird and, if there are any present, then reject that animal or bird.

If butchering your own stock, give it a good examination before slaughtering it.

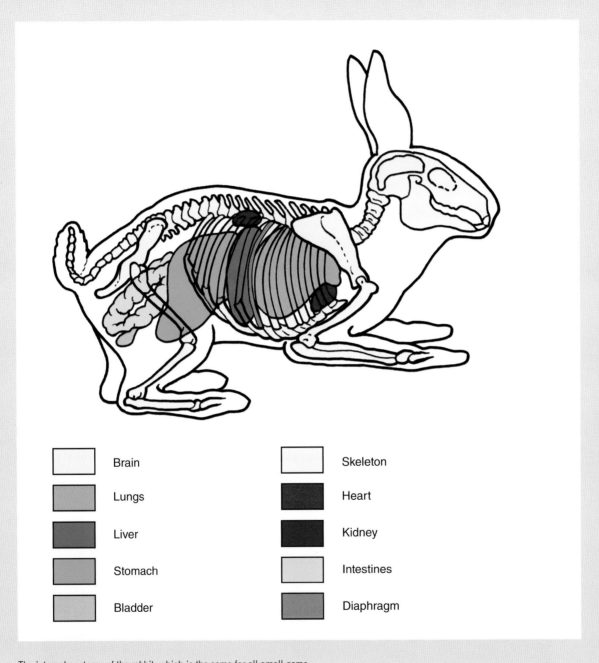

	Brain		Skeleton
	Lungs		Heart
	Liver		Kidney
	Stomach		Intestines
	Bladder		Diaphragm

The internal anatomy of the rabbit, which is the same for all small game.

Whilst examining the bird or animal internally, you should take note of the condition of the internal organs: are they the correct size and colour? Once you have butchered half a dozen healthy birds and the same number of small game, you will get to know what the organs should look like and be able to use this information as a reference; anything that does not conform to the normal condition should cause you to reject the animal or bird. It is not necessary for you to identify the disease that the animal or bird is carrying; you simply need to recognize internal signs of ill health. The liver should be studied very closely as it is a great indicator of the health of both birds and animals. If the liver is enlarged, shrivelled up, or pale in colour, instead of being deep red in appearance; or if it contains coloured spots, or has growths on it, then you have an indicator of ill health and the animal or bird should be rejected.

HYGIENE

There is not a great deal to say on this subject although it is, without doubt, one of the most, if not the most important, aspects of home butchering; if the working environment and practices are not clean and organized, the meat processed will be a potential source of food poisoning. Hygiene is easy to maintain, requiring no specialist skills, equipment, or knowledge; just a good measure of common sense and a bit of elbow grease.

Hygiene can be divided into four categories: personal hygiene, hygiene of the workspace, hygiene of the work tools, and hygienic

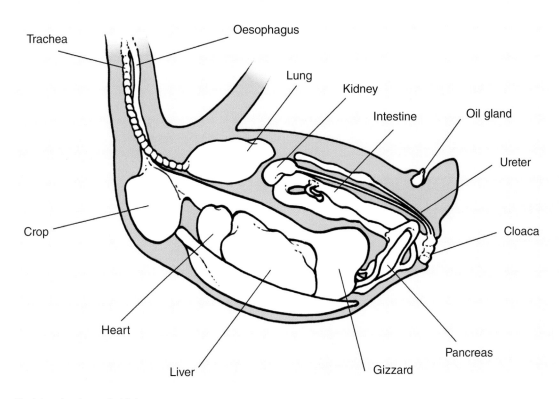

The internal anatomy of a bird.

Order is essential if good hygiene is to be practised. Have all your rabbits or birds lined up ready for processing.

practices. Personal hygiene is quite simply the maintenance of clean hands throughout the butchering process. The hands should be scrubbed like a surgeon's before starting the butchering and, whenever they become marked with blood or soiled in any way they should be rinsed in a bowl of warm water that should be present throughout the butchering process. The key to good butchering is clean hands, for two reasons: firstly, the hands provide numerous hiding places for all manner of bacteria that they come into contact with on a daily basis, so the cleaning of hands is essential to prevent this bacteria from contaminating good meat. Secondly, clean hands are better able to handle butchery tools dextrously, than dirty, slippery ones.

Hygiene of the workspace means keeping the butcher's bench clean, both before the butchering begins and during the butchering process; do not, for example, leave a pool of blood on your butcher's board and continue to work around it, but stop and clean away the blood with a cloth and warm water. Order is the key to a hygienic workstation; this means understanding all the processes that will take place and having containers ready to take the product produced by the butchering of an animal or bird. A chaotic workspace not only makes the butchering slower, it also makes it considerably less hygienic and such an approach will, sooner or later, lead to the production of meat that is not safe to eat.

The hygiene of the workspace also involves thoroughly cleaning up the work area at the

Keep your workbench clean and organized.

Organization means having clean containers, ready for all the parts of the rabbit or bird that will be produced by butchering. Here a bucket is used for the head and intestines of a rabbit, which will be used for ferret food. There is a bowl for the offal and another bowl containing the forelegs and hip section, which will be used for dog food. Finally, on the board, the meat from the loin and hind legs has been chopped and is ready to be soaked; the pelt has been folded neatly. Amazingly this is the produce of just one rabbit.

end of the butchering session: this means cleaning down your butchering boards with hot water and vinegar. Vinegar is antiseptic and prevents the growth of bacteria; it is also an organic way to clean your working environment. All the cloths that you use to clean up during the butchering process should be boiled to sterilize them, and any utensils used should be washed with hot water and vinegar.

Wherever you do your butchering, it must be a place that is completely free of vermin (rats and mice) as well as insects. If mice get into your butcher's workshop their droppings can cause salmonella and if rats get in the situation will be even worse: your workspace must therefore be 100 per cent vermin-proof.

With regard to the hygiene of work tools, such as knives and cleavers, these must not only be kept sharp, they must also be kept spotlessly clean – like surgical instruments – so that they do not become a source of meat contamination. Surgical instruments are sterilized because bacteria can attach themselves to the surface of a tool and enter the work area. All butchering tools should be

cleaned, both before and after butchering, using boiling water. Do not forget the handles: clean blades are of very little use if the handles are hosting a colony of bacteria.

The term 'hygienic practices' simply refers to a carefully planned approach to every stage of the butchering process: from the killing and hanging of birds and small game, to the plucking or skinning, and then onto the butchering and preserving of meat. Approach each of these

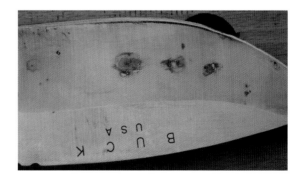

A knife like this will cause contamination of the meat and can lead to food poisoning.

All your knives should be kept clean and stored hygienically.

tasks in as clean and tidy a manner as possible and you will not go far wrong.

And finally, just a few words about the butcher's board, on which you will do all cutting and chopping. These can be either wood or plastic: if you opt for wood then you can make your own but, whatever their construction, you should have at least two, so that small game and birds can be butchered on separate boards, in order to prevent the possibility of cross-contamination. All butcher's boards should be scrubbed after use with hot water and vinegar, using a small scrubbing brush kept for the purpose. Boards will have cuts in their surface and these cuts, if not scrubbed clean, will become channels in which bacteria will establish themselves and multiply. Finally, do not forget to clean and scold the scrubbing brush after use, otherwise it will become a breeding ground for bacteria.

chapter four

The Butchering of Rabbits and Hares

PAUNCHING

The rabbit and the hare are of the same family: the lagomorphs. Consequently their general construction is the same and therefore they are both butchered in exactly the same manner, with the exception of the paunching process. The rabbit is paunched as soon as practically possible after death, whereas the hare is not paunched until it is being prepared for cooking, which means after a hanging period of eight or nine days.

The time at which the hare and the rabbit are paunched may be different, but the process of paunching is exactly the same in both animals. The paunch is most of the digestive tract including: the stomach, the large intestine and the small intestine. The stomach is located just within the last few ribs, nestling against the liver; the large and small intestines are located in the abdominal cavity.

The purpose of paunching is to remove the paunch intact, otherwise any damage caused to the delicate outer layer of the intestine or stomach will release semi-digested food or faeces that can taint the pelt, or contaminate the meat. It must also be remembered that the paunch of a hare that has hung for eight to nine days is in a state of decomposition; it is therefore in an extremely delicate condition. The contents of the intestine will have liquefied to a degree, so any damage to the paunch will release a semi-liquid material that will permeate the flesh of the hare before you have a chance to wash it away; so the paunching of the hare must be carried out with great delicacy.

If you paunch your rabbits at the end of your hunt, you must know what you are going to do with the pile of intestines that you end up with. If you have shot or ferreted ten rabbits this will mean a small bucket full of intestines; you do not want to leave them lying around near farm buildings or pathways as this will make you most unpopular with the farmer. Some hunters take a small spade along in their car and bury the paunches at the end of the hunt. I prefer to leave them under a hedgerow where they will provide food for wildlife; it doesn't take a crow with sharp eyes long to spot the offering, which will be greedily devoured; likewise a fox is not going to turn his nose up at a free meal.

If you paunch your rabbits at home, you must have a method of disposal for the paunches. I personally feed them to my ferrets, which tuck into the paunch of a rabbit with great enthusiasm but, if you do not have ferrets, the paunch must be got rid of in some other way. Simply placing them in your dustbin may not be acceptable: most councils have strict regulations about what they will and won't accept as rubbish and they may consider the paunch to be butcher's waste. You should therefore check with your local refuse department if you wish to get rid of the paunches via the dustbin. Burning the paunches may also land you in trouble if the council in your area has rules about bonfires.

Do not forget, however, that the paunch is made up of entirely natural, organic matter that will rot down and nourish the soil so, if you bury the paunches on your holding, they will, in time, fully decompose and improve the fertility of the soil.

1. To paunch a rabbit or hare, lay it on its back on a bench, or if no bench is available, lay it on the ground. Then, take a pinch of skin above the sternum of the last few ribs and place the tip of a filleting knife carefully into the pinch of skin, making sure you avoid your fingers. The reason you go in over the sternum, rather than going straight in over the abdominal cavity, is so that if you do happen to make a mistake and go too deep, instead of sending the tip of a very sharp knife right through the wall of the intestine, releasing its contents, you will strike the boney barrier of the sternum. The tip of the knife should not just pierce the skin, but also the flesh beneath, and the point should not be travelling in a downward direction, which is a common mistake made by the beginner, but in a rearward direction, towards the hind legs.

2. Once the tip is beneath the flesh, remove your fingers, releasing the pinch of skin and proceed very slowly and carefully along the abdomen, using the tip to do the work. The intestines are just below the skin and sometimes pressing right against it, so it is important that you have the tip of the blade under complete control at all times – like a surgeon making a precision opening. Though the tip of the blade is travelling in a rearward direction, there must also be constant upward pressure, which has the effect of drawing the flesh and skin of the abdomen up onto the edge of the blade, creating a small space between the back of the blade and the intestine beneath.

   During the course of making the incision, if the knife happens to lose contact for some reason (perhaps slipping to one side) and you need to restart, simply take a pinch of skin to the side of the incision you have already managed to make and pull it upwards. As you look down the line of the incision you will see that a gap has been made between the flesh of the abdomen and the intestine beneath. All you have to do to start again is place the point of your blade into that gap, release the pinch of skin and then proceed as before.

3. You now have an incision that stretches from the end of the ribcage and stops short of the hind legs, but this incision is presently too narrow to allow for the extraction of the paunch. Place the thumb of each hand into either side of the incision, midway down the cut with the fingers either side of the rabbit's spine. Now, lift the rabbit up and place it over a bucket, with its hind legs downward. Whilst maintaining pressure with your thumbs on either side of the incision, apply minimal force with the fingers on the spine, pushing forwards: you will see the intestine move forward slightly to protrude from the abdominal cavity.

4. Keep hold of the rabbit with just one hand – the left hand is best for right-handed people. Look at the paunch: the pale, kidney-shaped sack at the top of the paunch is the stomach; you need to place the thumb and first finger of the free hand, like a pincer, up under the last few ribs and find the top end of the stomach, which is attached to the liver. When you find this attachment, push up with the end of the thumb on the liver and down on the stomach with the first finger to force them apart. If you just pull on the stomach you will bring away about one third of the liver; you want to keep the liver intact as it is used for cooking and is delicious fried with onions, or added to other rabbit dishes such as rabbit pie or rabbit burgers. Cooks also prefer the liver intact, rather than torn into several pieces.

The paunching of a rabbit or hare begins by taking a small pinch of skin over the sternum near the last few ribs. Take a knife with a very fine point, such as a filleting knife, and place the tip of the point carefully into the pinch of skin. The point must not only pierce the skin itself, but also the flesh of the abdomen. Now make an incision in a rearward direction, towards the hind legs, whilst maintaining upward pressure with the cutting edge, throughout the course of the incision. The incision must also be straight, so do not allow the knife to wander to one side.

When the incision is complete, place one thumb in either side of the incision, with the fingers of each hand against the backbone of the rabbit. Hold the rabbit with its hind legs facing the ground, then pull gently with the thumbs and press against the rabbit's spine; you will see the intestines push forward out of the abdominal cavity.

Hold the rabbit in one hand and with the other hand reach into the abdominal cavity, with finger and thumb going underneath the ribcage to locate the point at which the stomach attaches to the liver. When this connection is located, push up with the thumb against the liver and down with the finger to break the connection.

Now pull the stomach forward then downward, towards the hind legs and the rest of the paunch will simply follow it.

Two paunched rabbits.

A healthy paunch, consisting of the stomach and the intestines.

5. Sometimes the stomach is attached to the liver and, in such cases, you will need to hold the liver in place with the left hand, while also still holding the rabbit in that hand and detaching the stomach carefully with the right hand. Once the stomach and the liver are separated, move the thumb and first finger round behind the stomach and form them into a pincer, encircling the stomach not gripping it. It is important that you do not grip the stomach in the middle as pressure at this point may rupture the stomach wall and release the contents; this is particularly important in the case of a hare that has been hanging for eight to nine days.

6. With the stomach cupped between the first finger and thumb, pull it forward and downward and then let it simply drop into the bucket. The weight of the stomach will then pull the intestines cleanly out of the abdominal cavity. Keep an eye on the kidneys as the intestines fall forward, as occasionally the intestines will draw a kidney down with them: the kidneys like the liver are a valuable piece of offal with a good flavour.

7. The paunch will now be hanging by the single piece of intestine that leads to the rabbit's pelvic bone; all you have to do to completely detach the paunch is pull on this piece of intestine. Now only one tiny length of intestine remains: this is located within the pelvic bone and ends at the anus. Many people find the removal of this piece of intestine unpleasant, but it has to be done; this small piece of intestine contains about half a dozen rabbit droppings and, whilst eating one of these droppings is most unlikely to do you any harm, the appearance of rabbit droppings on the plate whilst eating is most off-putting. I once looked at a rabbit that someone was boiling and there

were rabbit droppings floating around in the bubbling water; it transpired that the person doing the cooking had not removed the intestine from the pelvic bone, hence the droppings.

8. To remove the intestine from the pelvic bone, simply push your finger through the cavity that exists down the centre of the pelvic bone from inside the rabbit, until the end of your finger appears just below the rabbit's tail. As you do this, you will see droppings being forced out; the small piece of intestine will then appear. There is no need for a knife, simply pull this piece of intestine and it will come away easily. If you find this task unpleasant, then wear a surgical glove to do the job.

The paunch of a rabbit, and especially the paunch of a hare that has been hanging for some time, has a distinct smell that many people find objectionable and this smell transfers readily to the hands during the paunching process. To avoid this you can wear surgical gloves, which protect the hands from the smell, whilst still allowing more than enough manual dexterity to perform the task.

However, I prefer not to wear gloves, as it seems to me that the introduction of rubber gloves to this very natural and earthy process is somewhat alien. If you do not wear gloves to paunch a rabbit, then a natural soap containing lavender and chamomile will take care of the smell very efficiently. When you first begin paunching rabbits, have a bowl of warm water close by that has 1tbsp (10ml) of vinegar added to it, and a clean cloth that has been sterilized in boiling water. If you do happen to cut the intestine with your knife and some of the contents get onto the flesh inside the abdominal cavity, complete the paunching as quickly as you can, then thoroughly wash out the abdominal cavity with the sterile cloth and vinegar water.

SKINNING

Now that you have removed the intestine of the rabbit or hare, it is time to turn your attention to removing the skin. Many people simply discard the skin, which is a waste, so they take very little care over its removal. However, as you will see from Chapter 7, the skin of the rabbit or hare is extremely useful and can be used to make a range of items including: garments, rugs, bed coverings and bags. I will show you how to skin a rabbit in such a way that the skin is kept intact and in prime condition. The aim is to remove the skin in one piece, from the hocks of the hind legs, to the knuckles of the front legs, and all the way up the neck to the ears of the rabbit or hare. It is even possible for a person with good knife skills to remove the skin from the rabbit or hare's head with the ears still attached.

The entire rabbit skin, with the ears still attached, can be achieved by the skilled skinner.

Skinning a Rabbit

1. To begin the skinning process, go to the back end of the incision made for paunching, then take a pinch of skin on one of the hind legs and place your knife point in the pinch of skin; make an incision all the way up the inside of the leg right to the hock. As you near the hock, the skin becomes too tight for the blade to continue to work from underneath, so you must proceed with the incision from the outside, using your knife in the scalpel hold. When you have finished, you should have a straight incision up the inside of the leg that meets the incision along the abdomen. Any small-bladed, sharp knife is suitable for the opening of the skin along the hind leg but I find a small filleting knife the most efficient for this task.
2. Once the incision is completed along the inside of one hind leg, repeat the process along the other hind leg. I make the incision along the inside of the hind leg

from the outside, rather than cutting the skin from underneath. Cutting from the outside, using the knife like a scalpel, is easier than cutting from underneath, but it requires a high degree of knife skill as you have to cut through the skin, which is thinner than paper, and not cut the flesh of the leg beneath. Such knife skills take time to acquire, but when you are up to the task, working along the outside of the hind leg is easier than working from underneath the skin and makes a better cut.

3. Return to the paunching incision and you will notice that there is a lip of flesh along either side of the incision. Take hold of the lip of flesh on one side of the incision firmly, using your fingers and thumb. You want to do this to the rear of the incision, close to the hind legs. Now, with your other hand, pull the skin away from the flesh; as this happens you will notice a membrane appear that attaches the skin to the flesh. You need to place your thumb underneath this membrane and, as you pull on the skin, push in the opposite direction on the

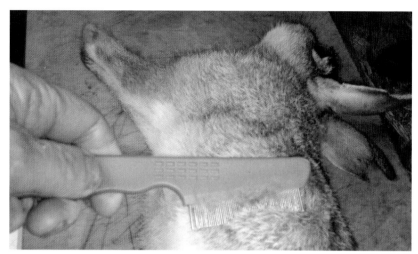

Before skinning, groom the rabbit.

BELOW: The skinning process begins by making a straight incision up the inside of the hind leg, which stretches from the paunching incision to the hock.

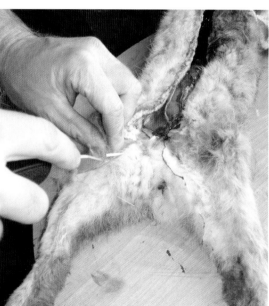

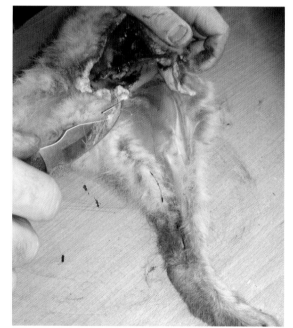

membrane with the thumb, whilst working it up and down to detach it completely from the skin.

This job can be done with a knife, but I find the thumb better suited to the task. On the initial pull to separate the skin from the flesh, at the rear of the paunching incision, a reasonable amount of force is required when dealing with rabbits, but on hares that have been hanging for eight or nine days care should be exercised as the flesh is very tender and, if you pull on it too firmly, you will simply pull it to pieces.

4. If at any point during the skinning process you see flesh being peeled away with the skin, stop what you are doing and get your thumb behind the peeling flesh and work it away from the skin. Alternatively, take a

Along the paunching incision you will note a pinkish lip of belly flesh. Hold this lip firmly and pull the skin away from the flesh, along the side of the rabbit.

broad-bladed skinning knife and get the edge of the blade behind the peel of flesh and very carefully cut it away from the skin. Some people will tell you to use a blunt knife for the skinning process, to prevent you from cutting through the skin, which is a ludicrous suggestion; a blunt knife is nothing more than a crude, ineffective edge that is less efficient than using the side of the thumb. When a knife is required to make a cut that has a blunt edge, you will force the blade because it does not work as easily and you will simply end up pushing it right through the skin.

To work smoothly and with little effort a knife must be razor sharp; any knife used in the skinning process must therefore be extremely sharp, so that it glides along easily, and is easy to control. If you find it difficult to work the lip of flesh along the paunching incision away from the skin, then use a broad-bladed skinning knife with a very sharp edge that has been along a sharpening steel to do the job. Do not use the point of the blade to separate the skin from the flesh as this leads to more pierced skins than anything else; use the curved portion of the blade,

making short, precise movements, proceeding down between the skin and flesh, getting the knife behind the connective membrane.

5. Now that the hind leg has an incision all the way to the hock, there is only one more operation required before the skin can be removed from the hind legs: that is to make a circular cut all the way around the hock joint. Next, take hold of the skin on one side of the incision, along the inside of the hind leg, between fingers and thumb and pull it back slightly. Then place the end of the thumb underneath the skin, working it back and forth to detach the skin from the flesh beneath. Continue this operation, working in a circular direction from one side of the incision, around the leg, to the other side of the incision.

6. To use the thumb to separate the skin from the flesh around the hind leg requires a strong thumb that is accustomed to manual labour. If your thumb is not strong enough then you will need to use a knife; the best kind of knife for this work is a small skinner, like the Buck caping knife mentioned earlier. When pulling back the skin along the edge of the incision to give the thumb, or the knife, access to separate the skin and the flesh, do not pull too hard or you will find that you inadvertently pull back a large flap of skin and bring away with it a piece of leg meat. This is especially true of a hare that has been hanging: pull on the skin of a hare too violently and you will rip off large pieces of tender leg meat, making a mess of this valuable joint.

7. The membrane attaching the skin to the flesh of the hind leg is very tenacious and it must be teased away with the thumb, or cut away with the knife. I have seen books that depict the ripping of the skin away from the hind leg: no teasing, no use of the thumb, no cutting with the knife, just a violent ripping away, which is very amateurish. More importantly, it will tear away pieces of leg meat, so ignore such books

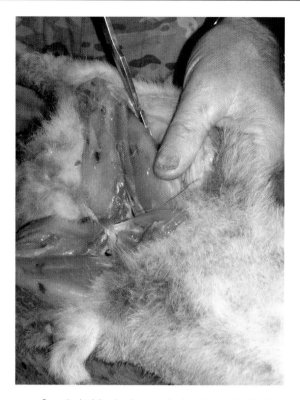

Take hold of the end of the skin and pull it upward, towards the tail and as the connective membrane appears, get your thumb behind it and work it away from the skin. Repeat the process with the other leg, so that the skin is ready to be detached at the base of the tail, and proceed as described in the text.

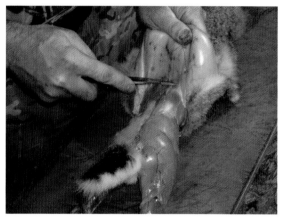

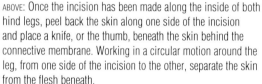

ABOVE: Once the incision has been made along the inside of both hind legs, peel back the skin along one side of the incision and place a knife, or the thumb, beneath the skin behind the connective membrane. Working in a circular motion around the leg, from one side of the incision to the other, separate the skin from the flesh beneath.

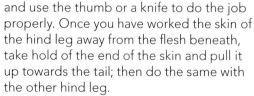

RIGHT: Pull the skin down the back, towards the head, and if it becomes difficult, use a knife to free it.

and use the thumb or a knife to do the job properly. Once you have worked the skin of the hind leg away from the flesh beneath, take hold of the end of the skin and pull it up towards the tail; then do the same with the other hind leg.

8. The skin now has to be detached from the tail: this is achieved by pushing a blade under the skin at the base of the tail, with the cutting edge facing the tail. Then turn the blade until it achieves an angle of roughly 30 degrees, at which point you can cut through the skin, freeing it from the tail. If the angle of cut is too shallow you will strip the fur from the tail; this is not a good idea because the tail is used for making such items as the rabbit's tail version of a feather duster; the tails can also be used to embellish clothing made from rabbit skin.

9. The skin is now ready to be pulled down the spine and over the ribs of the rabbit. To achieve this all you do is take firm hold of the end of the skin and pull it down the

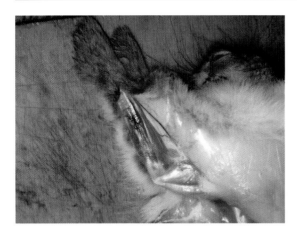

When the skin is pulled down the spine and over the shoulder blades, it is time to remove the skin from the front legs. First take hold of a front foot and push on it, placing pressure against the inside of the skin around the elbow, causing the elbow and upper part of the leg to come free from the skin. Once this is achieved, cut through the skin on the underside of the leg all the way to the knee joint above the toes, then make a circular cut around the knee joint and fold back the skin.

spine towards the head, whilst gripping the rabbit's loins firmly in the other hand. You should clearly see as the skin progresses down the spine, the skin coming cleanly away from the connective membrane beneath. However, if it doesn't and the membrane starts to come away with the skin, stop pulling and get a knife blade behind the membrane and cut it away from the skin, then continue to pull the skin towards the head.

10. When you reach the shoulders of the rabbit, you should stop pulling. Move to the other side of the skin and take hold of one of the front feet; then with the other hand, use the first finger and thumb to push against the inside of the skin around the elbow joint. Then push on the rabbit's foot and you will see the elbow and upper part of the front leg push backwards out of the skin. Push the foot as far as it will go; then take a very sharp knife with a fine point and cut through the skin of the front leg, coming from the underside of the leg, cutting all the way down to the knuckle joint located just above the toes. Make a circular cut around the knuckle joint; then remove the skin from the front leg with the thumb or a knife, in the same way as you removed the skin from the hind leg. Repeat this process on the other front leg.

11. Once again, take hold of the skin and pull it down the neck and as far up the head as it will go. If your rabbit was killed by delivering a neck chop, there will be a lot of blood in the neck area and, as the skin moves forwards, it might cause the rupturing of the blood-soaked flesh or vessels around the neck, causing dark blood to run out. You can be prepared for this by having several balls of cotton wool, about the size of a pea, standing by. Locate the source of the bleed and pack it with the small balls of cotton wool, which will stem the flow and prevent blood getting on the pelt. This also keeps your work surface nice and clean as nothing makes more mess than lots of sticky blood all over your workbench.

12. Lay the rabbit on its back and draw an imaginary line down the centre of the neck to the nose; then place the tip of a very sharp knife through the skin that is now pulled back beneath the cheek bones and make a cut in the direction of the nose, along the imaginary line that you have drawn. Return to the starting point of this cut and then work in a circular direction, with the tip of your knife working over the cheeks, cutting away the skin from the flesh and detaching it from the rabbit's face, just short of the eyes. Working upwards slightly, still in a circular fashion, separate the skin from the flesh and then detach the skin at the base of the ear. Now go to the other side of the rabbit's face and repeat the process: the end result will be the complete removal of the skin in one piece.

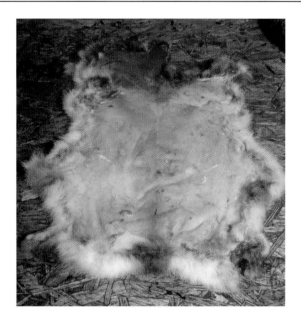

LEFT: Repeat this process on the other front leg and then the skin can be pulled over the head and cut away, as described in the text, leaving you with the pelt.

ABOVE: Fold the detached skin, flesh-to-flesh, then fur-to-fur.

To keep the skin in good order whilst you carry out the butchering of the rabbit, lay it fur-side down and then fold it in half, skin-to-skin, then fold it in half again, fur-to-fur, and place it to one side to be dealt with as explained in Chapter 7. Do not place salt on the skin as suggested by some books: the use of salt was only used in the past for the preservation of skins if they were to be transported to another place for curing; it is, therefore, not necessary for the home curer to salt. If you apply salt to the skins during the damp, cool months of winter when curing takes place, the salt draws in the moisture and turns the skin into a soggy mess – at least, that was my experience in the early days when I was learning the craft, following books that told me to salt green skins.

The rabbit is now without a skin, apart from the tail, some skin on the feet and some on the front of the head. Let us turn our attention to getting rid of this remaining skin and hair, starting with the tail. This is achieved by making a V-shaped cut, produced by two angled cuts firstly down one side of the tail base, then repeated at the same angle on the other side of the tail base. The tail will now fold forward and a cut across the base will detach it cleanly from the rabbit. If there is any flesh on the base of the tail, cut it away and then place the tail to one side to be dealt with, as outlined in Chapter 7. If meat is left attached to the tail it will decompose and make the tail unusable, so make sure that it is all removed; however, the bone down the centre of the tail stays.

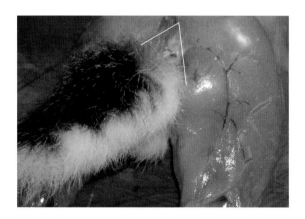

To remove the tail, make a V-shaped cut, formed by two angled cuts one either side of the tail. Fold the tail forward and cut it away at the base. Remove any flesh still attached to the base of the tail.

Now turn your attention to the feet, which should be removed using a small cleaver. Start with the larger hind feet, removing them above the hock joint with one single blow, allowing the weight of the cleaver to do the work. The cleaver will cut cleanly through the bone and the flesh with ease, if it is sharp and is used correctly. You do not need to raise the cleaver above your head like some mad axe man, very little force is required to chop off the feet; simply place the cleaver over the point at which you intend to chop, then raise the cleaver up from the wrist and strike at that point. Your eyes should be focused on the point you intend to strike and not on the cleaver. Whatever you do, don't hold the foot close to the hock joint as a miscalculation on your part could end up with you losing a finger; hold the foot right down by the toes. If the bone is shattered and jagged after the chop then the cleaver is not sharp enough, or if it is sharp, it is not heavy enough.

Once both hind feet have been chopped away, turn your attention to the front ones: these need to be chopped away well above the knee joint, using the same controlled, single blow to remove them as you used on

To remove the hind feet: place the rabbit or hare on one side, hold the foot close to the toes and extend the leg, whilst keeping it in full contact with the chopping board. Place your cleaver over the intended strike point, which should be about ¼in (6mm) above the hock joint. Raise the cleaver from the wrist about 4in (10cm) above the mark and, keeping your eyes fixed on the strike point, make one cut that should cleanly sever the hind foot. Now turn your attention to the front feet and give them the same treatment, severing them ¼in (6mm) above the knee joint.

the hind feet. Unfortunately, there is no use for the rabbit's feet, other than keeping one as a lucky charm if you happen to believe in such superstitions. You could burn them, then grind them down using a pestle and mortar and scatter the ground down bone over your vegetable plot to improve the soil.

Removing the head is another job for the trusty cleaver. Place the rabbit on its side and hold its head by the nose; then place the cleaver over the point you intend to strike (which should be just back from the base of the skull), raise the cleaver, again from the wrist, and deliver a single blow that should cut through the neck flesh and completely sever the bone. If the rabbit has been killed by a neck chop, then remove the head slightly behind the area of neck that has been bloodied and bruised by the blow.

If you wish you could make use of the rabbit's head by carefully removing the remaining skin and hair with the tip of a sharp knife, cut off the ears and boil the head until the flesh is soft, at which point it will flake easily off the bone. The skull can then be cut open with a small hacksaw and the brains removed. The flesh of the head and the brain can then be used as dog meat, which dogs absolutely adore. You could give your dog the eyes as well, although most people are too squeamish to prise them out.

Using every part of the rabbit in this way is not only good stewardship of the resources, but it also makes sound economic sense. If you do not have a dog, then you could skin the head and boil it to make a stock for gravies or soups. If you think that the head cannot be used then think again: Mrs Beeton, the famous Victorian cook, used to roast rabbits and hares with the head still on and the cheeks were a particular favourite with diners.

REMOVING THE OFFAL

The next task is to retrieve the offal from inside the rabbit: this consists of the liver, two kidneys and the heart, all of which are perfectly edible and truly delicious. To access the offal, lay the rabbit on its back and pull back the opening in the abdomen; you will then see, slightly behind the ribcage, the dark red liver and nestled up tightly against either side of the spine, surrounded by a small fat deposit, the kidneys.

1. To remove the liver, simply reach in to the top of the abdominal cavity with finger and thumb and feel around the sides of the liver until you are behind it, at which point you should be able to locate its attachment to the diaphragm. When this is located, pull the attachment away and the liver will then come away in your hand easily.

2. The liver is made up of several lobes and where the lobes meet there is a duct that secretes bile, a yellow or greenish liquid that is used in the duodenum to aid digestion. Bile is a bitter-tasting substance and so the bile duct is supposed to be removed because, if it is left in, it is said that it will make the liver taste bitter. However, I have eaten many a rabbit liver from which the bile duct was not removed and I have to say that it made no difference whatsoever to the taste of the liver. There was no hint of bitterness and, in fact, the livers with the bile duct still in place were perfectly delicious; I am therefore of the opinion that removing the bile duct from small game is a total waste of time, especially as it is such a fiddly job.

    I have read articles by people who tell you that you can simply pinch out the bile duct with the finger and thumb and wondered if they have ever actually removed one from a rabbit's liver; it has to be carefully excised with the point of a sharp knife. Remove the bile duct if you must, but I shall not be going into the procedure, as I consider it to be a total waste of time.

    When removing the liver from a hare that has been hung, a good degree of care must be exercised because the liver will have become very tender during the hanging process and will tear easily.

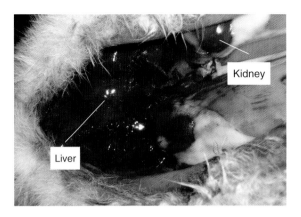

The liver is located inside the abdominal cavity, just behind the ribcage, up against the diaphragm. The kidneys are located in the loin region of the rabbit or hare, nestled tightly up below the spine, surrounded by a deposit of fat.

3. To remove the kidneys, simply peel them away from the side of the spine with the fat that encases them. Remove the fat from the kidney but do not discard it as it can be chopped up and added to burgers and pies. To locate the heart, look inside the abdominal cavity; at the end of the ribs you will see a wall of skin stretched right across the ribs, sealing the chest cavity: this is called the diaphragm. Make an incision in the diaphragm, then reach in as far as your hand will go and feel about; you should soon be able to feel the unmistakable shape of the heart and also the lungs. Take a good grip on both the heart and lungs and pull them out of the chest cavity. Separate the heart from the lungs and use the lungs as dog food.

REMOVING SHOT

Some rabbits and hares will have been shot with a shotgun and consequently there may be pieces of shot lodged in the flesh of the animal, which will, of course, have to be removed prior to cooking. For the procedure on the finding and removal of shot refer to the relevant section in Chapter 5.

BRINE SOAKING THE MEAT

You now have a carcase of rabbit or hare meat that can be treated in a number of different ways, depending on what you intend to cook. If you are roasting the meat then no further butchery is required, other than to truss the carcase, which serves to keep it in shape and retain any stuffing you place within the rabbit or hare. If you are going to make rabbit stew or fried rabbit, then you will want to cut the rabbit up into portions that are still on the bone; while for burgers, rabbit pies, game pies and curries you will want to remove the flesh from the bone and cut it into bite-sized chunks.

Whatever option you go for – whole carcase, cuts on the bone or diced pieces – they must all spend roughly two hours soaking in a bowl of cold water to which 1tbsp (25g) of salt and 2tbsp (20ml) of white vinegar have been added.

The purpose of soaking the meat in brine is four-fold: firstly to remove excess bodily fluids from the vascular system. Secondly, to loosen surface tissue, which is tough and unpleasant to eat; this tissue will simply rub away with a clean tea towel when the meat is removed from the brine. Thirdly, to lightly tenderize the meat, which is important when cooking older rabbits or hares with tougher flesh: the cook will find that a rabbit or hare that has been soaked in brine will be lighter and tastier. Some cooks believe that soaking the meat will bleach it, taking away the flavour, but this is not the case, in fact quite the opposite is true. The flesh of older rabbits or hares can be very tough and unpleasant to eat if it is not well prepared but soaking the flesh in brine overnight will have a dramatic tenderizing effect, turning tough flesh into light, rich and tasty meat. Finally, soaking the rabbit or hare in brine will remove the many hairs that have, inevitably, stuck to the flesh during the skinning process.

AGEING RABBITS AND HARES

This seems like an appropriate moment to look at the task of ageing a rabbit or hare; it is essential for the cook to have this information, so that they can decide how to prepare the meat. The meat of an old, wild rabbit or hare can either be delicious and rich in taste, or it can be like eating cotton wool and chewing gum simultaneously: what makes the difference is the preparation. The meat of a young rabbit or hare on the other hand is light and tender; personally I do not think it has the depth of flavour found in an older animal, although it is certainly easier to prepare. Farmed rabbits are all going to be young and tender but wild rabbits or hares can be anything from six months to many years old – the older the animal, the tougher the flesh.

So how do your tell the age of a rabbit or hare? Size is the first indicator: young rabbits and hares are smaller than older ones. The size of wild rabbits and hares varies throughout the country; the rabbits that I harvest in Scotland with ferrets and a gun are much bigger than the rabbits I used to take in Cambridgeshire. However, once you have butchered your first few dozen rabbits or hares, you will soon get to know what constitutes the average-sized, full-grown rabbit or hare and what constitutes a younger animal.

On closer inspection you will discover that the ears are a good indicator of age; the ears of a young rabbit or hare will be fresh and will be shorter, rounder and thinner than a full-grown rabbit or hare. With the older rabbit or hare the ears are bigger, on males they will be ragged and torn from fighting and on both males and females they will be thicker. Teeth also give an indication of age: the young rabbit or hare will have gleaming white teeth that are not in the least worn, whereas old rabbits or hares have worn and discoloured teeth.

When you start skinning rabbits and hares you will soon notice that the skin of a young rabbit or hare is very much thinner than the skin of an older animal, sometimes paper thin, and there is considerably less fat on the skin than there is on an older animal. When you open up the rabbit or hare you will discover that the younger animal has a smaller liver and kidney than an older one. Old rabbits or hares also have a much heavier fat deposit along the inside of the back; in very old animals this stretches from the front of the loin to the rump and is very dense. It is an important role of the butcher to identify the age and also the condition of the animal being prepared, so that this information can be passed onto the person who is doing the cooking, so that they can prepare the meat in the correct way.

I shall not go into the specifics of cooking the meat of older rabbit and hares: this is a book on butchery and not one on cooking after all. However, I do not consider the soaking in brine to be a cookery task but a butchery one and, although an overnight soaking is very effective at tenderizing the flesh, do not get carried away; the maximum soaking period is twenty-four hours, any longer than this and the very structure of the meat may start to break down and begin to shrivel up.

TRUSSING

Trussing is required when a rabbit or hare is going to be roasted. Trussing provides two functions: firstly it keeps the stuffing in the animal's abdominal cavity; secondly, it preserves the animal's shape during the roasting process.

When rabbit or hare are roasted they are normally stuffed with a forcemeat made from sausage, liver, onion and spices, to which may well be added some form of fat. Quite a lot of forcemeat is inserted, which would come out during the cooking process, unless the meat was trussed, as the skin along the abdomen shrinks due to the heat. To prevent this from happening, once the forcemeat is in place, the abdomen is sewn up using a needle and string. The string must be removed before the rabbit or hare is served, as you do not want people to be chewing on thread as they eat.

You will need an upholstery needle to sew up the abdomen.

To truss a rabbit or hare the hind legs are pushed forwards and the forelegs are pushed backwards, so that they lie along the side of the animal's body, allowing the roast to sit flat in the roasting tray. To keep the legs in place you can drive a skewer through the leg and into the body of the rabbit or hare, which requires four skewers, or you can simply tie the legs in place with a length of string that goes over the legs and around the body.

CUTTING THE RABBIT OR HARE INTO JOINTS

For dishes such as stew and fried rabbit or hare, and for preserving the meat of the rabbit or hare, the carcase has to be cut into manageable sized pieces. The carcase is therefore divided up into the following cuts: the forelegs, generally referred to as the shoulder because the bulk of the meat is in the shoulder area; the front legs are removed whole to make this cut and you obviously end up with two portions. The hind legs, simply referred to as the legs, are again removed in one piece and provide two portions. The loin, which is the section between the ribcage and the hind legs, provides just one portion, unless you split it down the middle along the spine using a saw. The meat along the loin is the most tender of all the meat on the rabbit and is also the tastiest. The final cut is the rump, which is quite simply the rear end of the rabbit to which the hind legs are attached and it provides just one portion.

A good-sized rabbit divided in this way will serve three people, if divided up as follows. Serving one: one leg and half the loin. Serving two: one leg and the rump. Serving three: two shoulders and half a loin. On a large animal like a sheep or pig you would make use of the ribcage and the neck, the ribcage providing a rack from which rib chops are taken and the neck making a substantial joint. However, the ribcage and neck on the rabbit yield such a

An alternative skinning method. Begin by cutting off the head.

Cut off the front feet.

Cut off the hind feet.

Cut the skin away from the hind leg.

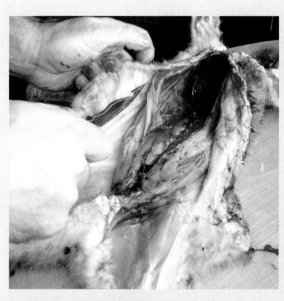

Free the skin from the belly and ribcage.

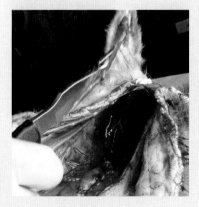

Free the skin from the front leg.

Peel the skin down the side of the rabbit and over the spine; then repeat the process from the other side.

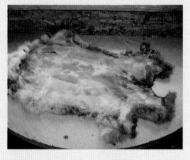

The removed pelt.

small amount of meat that they are not worth preparing, other than to be used for making a good stock.

However, two nice small fillets can be taken from the top of the ribs and these are worth removing, as they are extremely tender and good for frying. The ribcage can be fed to dogs, but only to those who have been reared on such a diet; but the ribcage, as with all rabbit scraps on the bone must be fed fresh, never cooked. If you cook the ribcage, or any other portion containing rabbit bone, the bone will become brittle and will shatter when the dog chews it, presenting a potential hazard that could result in mouth injuries or damage to the intestine. This is not the case with the raw bone, and dogs brought up on this kind of diet are able to chew and digest it with no problem.

1. Let us now take a look at how to produce the above cuts of rabbit or hare meat, beginning with the shoulder. The shoulder is attached to the side of the rabbit or hare by muscle alone, unlike the human arm, which has a bone connection in the form of a joint; therefore, when detaching the shoulder there is no bone around which you have to manipulate the knife. To remove the shoulder, take hold of the

leg below the elbow and push it back and up, until the shoulder blade raises away from the side of the rabbit or hare. At this point, place the cutting edge of your knife behind the shoulder blade and make a clean cut, right across the back of the shoulder blade, towards the neck, keeping the blade of the knife against the side of the rabbit or hare throughout the cut.

2. With the front legs removed to make the shoulder cut, it is time to remove the back legs to make the cut simply known as the leg. The back legs, unlike the front ones, are attached by a ball and socket joint to the pelvic bone. The ball end of this joint is at the top end of the hind leg and the socket part of the joint is located in the pelvic bone. It is important that you understand this description because you will need to identify this joint at the top of the hind leg, in order to steer the knife deftly around it.

    With the rabbit or hare lying on its back, begin by drawing an imaginary line across the top of the hind leg from the inside. When you have this line well worked out, cut along it from the front of the hind leg, making the cut the full depth of the thigh. Half way across the leg you will come to bone, at which point stop cutting and

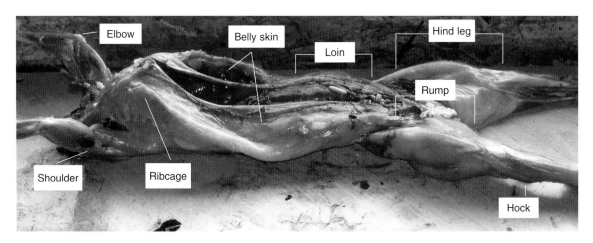

The carcase waiting to be butchered.

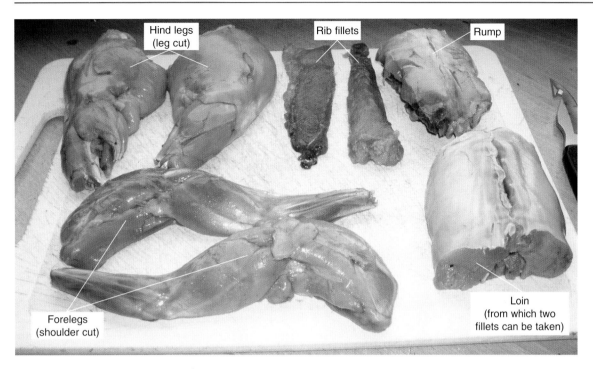

The carcase of a rabbit divided into cuts.

repeat the process, coming from the back of the hind leg. This cut is best made with a substantial blade, as a thinner bladed knife, such as a filleting knife, does not have the strength for such work.

Now apply pressure to the base of the pelvic bone to hold the rabbit or hare in place; with the other hand, take hold of the hind leg that you have just cut around and push it forcibly down until you hear a definite popping sound, which is the sound of the ball part of the ball and socket joint popping out of the socket. If the joint does not pop when the animal is on its back, then turn it on its side and apply pressure to the leg until the joint does pop.

When the joint has popped, place your knife blade back in the cut you made along the top of the hind leg and follow the cut back in, until you come to the joint. Now, take hold of the end of the hind leg and manipulate it until you can see the ball part of the joint; when you identify it, guide

To make the cut known as the shoulder, manipulate the front leg so that the shoulder blade moves away from the side of the rabbit or hare; then place a knife behind it and make a clean cut right across the back of the shoulder, towards the neck.

65

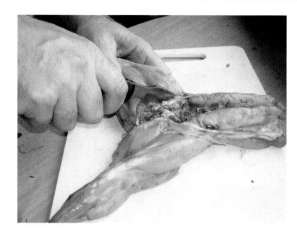

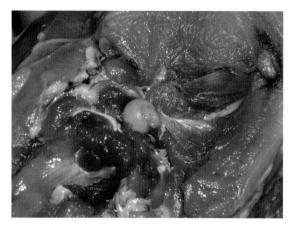

To remove the hind leg for the cut simply known as the leg, place the rabbit or hare on its back and cut through the flesh at the top of the leg from the front until you come to bone. Do the same, this time cutting from the back.

Take hold of the hind leg and force it downward, until you hear a popping sound. This is the sound of the ball part of the ball and socket joint popping out of the socket.

Send your knife back down the front cut and then manipulate the leg until the ball portion of the joint is made visible. Then guide the knife around the ball and into the cut on the other side.

You now have your first leg, however there is just one more task to complete in order to finish the job off: the removal of the tendon's anchor point, which is attached to the muscle at the back of the lower part of the hind leg. The tendon is easily identifiable as it is creamy white in colour and looks like a strong rubber band. Simply cut up the muscle along the side of the tendon until you come to the top of the tendon; cut across it and down the other side, thus removing it. If you leave this tendon in place and someone eats it, they will end up chewing on something that resembles a piece of rubber, has no taste and is not easy to digest.

your knife up and around the ball and into the cut on the other side of the leg. There is a bit of a knack to this manipulation of the knife around the ball part of the joint, but it will not take too much practice before you get the hang of it.

3. To produce the loin cut, first lay the rabbit or hare on its back and trim away the belly skin. Some people use the belly skin but I think it is a poor quality part of the rabbit or hare that is tough and difficult to chew – a bit like jerky. To cut away the belly skin, follow the natural line of the skin from the hind legs to the ribcage with the edge of a sharp knife. Next, cut through both sides of the loin meat, just behind the ribs and just in front of the rump.

To produce the cut known as the loin, begin by placing the rabbit or hare on its back and removing the belly skin.

Make a cut through the loin meat, at the back of the ribcage and the front of the rump, taking the cut all the way down to the backbone.

All that remains is to sever the bone at the front and rear of the loin to separate this cut of meat from the carcase. There are two ways to go about this: you can use a saw (a simple hacksaw that has been sterilized will do the job) or you can use a cleaver. For the beginner, the hacksaw will do the neatest job, but for those who are proficient in the use of the cleaver, it is an easy job to chop clean through the relatively thin backbone of a rabbit or hare with one precise blow. However, if you miss the intended mark and strike the loin meat, which is very tender, you will make a mess of it. Finally, run your thumb over the loin cut which will cause the covering membrane to come away; this needs to be peeled off or it will cause the meat to be stringy.

4. The cut known as the rump has now been produced as a result of removing the hind legs and the loin: simply trim off any straggly bits of membrane or meat and it is ready.

Sever the loin from the back of the ribcage and front of the rump. Now rub your finger over the loin and you will disturb a thin surface membrane that is tough and transparent. This needs to be removed from both loins by pulling it away.

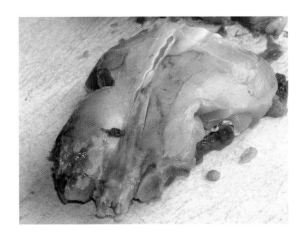

The rump cut.

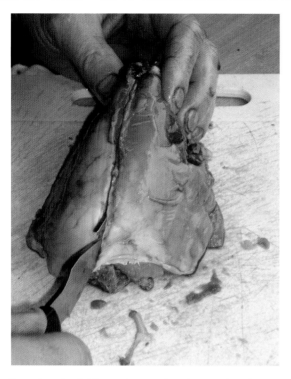

To produce the rib fillets, make a cut along the spine from the neck stump to the back of the ribcage.

Follow the cut down and over the rib bones until the fillet comes away.

5. The last cut to be made is the rib fillets, removed from along the top of the ribcage. To remove these make a cut along the spine, from the point where the neck joins the spine to the end of the ribcage. Rub your finger over the fillets and, as with the loin, you will find that you disturb a membrane that needs to be removed. Carefully work a knife down the cut you have made, from the spine towards the top of the ribcage, making sure that you stay in contact with the spine and then the bones of the ribcage. As you make this cut the tender rib fillet will simply come away. Repeat on the other side.

If making a curry or a pie that requires the meat to be removed from the bone, the process is very straightforward, if somewhat fiddly. To remove the loin from the bone, simply make a cut along the spine and place your thumb in behind the loin and work it from one end to the other and the meat will simply fall away in most cases. If the rabbit or hare is somewhat older and the loin meat is a bit reluctant to come away from the bone, simply use the side of a sharp knife to remove it.

To remove the meat from the legs, start by standing a leg on end and you will see the ball part of the ball and socket joint, beneath it you will see some tendons attaching the muscle to the bone. Place your knife blade in front of these tendons and then cut through the flesh shallowly. Go under the tendons until you come to the bone, then turn your knife and follow the bone down to the hock joint, cutting through one side of the hind leg as you go. Return to the top of the bone, just beneath the ball joint,

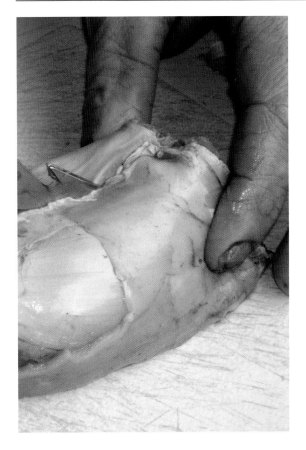

To remove the loin from the bone, make a cut along the side of the spine; place the thumb in behind the cut and ease the loin meat away from the bone.

and work the knife down and around the bone, removing all the meat from the bone until you come to the hock joint.

On the front of the hock joint you will find a tendon connection, holding the muscle to the bone. You need to move your knife over, around and underneath this tendon connection; when this is achieved, work your knife down and around the bone to remove the meat from the lower portion of the bone. When you get really good at this the meat will come away in one piece, but it really does not matter if the meat comes away in two or three pieces as it's all going to be chopped up anyway.

Some people will remove the meat from the shoulder and the rump with the knife; personally I find this a waste of time, as the amount of meat that can be cleaned from these cuts with the knife is so small that it is not worth the effort. These cuts are best suited to dishes where the meat can be cooked on the bone.

chapter five

The Butchering of Birds both Domestic and Wild

INTRODUCTION

It does not matter whether it is a wild pheasant, mallard or goose or a domestically reared chicken or guinea fowl: the butchery process is the same, the only difference being the amount of time required to hang the bird correctly. Even the smaller birds, pigeon, quail, partridge and snipe, are butchered in exactly the same manner as the giant turkeys and geese, except that the larger birds take much longer to process in comparison to the smaller ones. In this chapter we shall use the chicken as our example, but everything that you see and read about the butchering of the chicken is relevant to the butchering of all other types of birds; big or small, domestically reared or wild. The reason I have selected the chicken to feature in this chapter is because it is the backbone of every smallholding throughout the country and it is the bird that the smallholder is therefore most likely to be butchering.

AGEING BIRDS AND HANGING TIMES FOR DIFFERENT SPECIES OF BIRD

You will already know that the hanging process, as previously described in relation to small game, is carried out in order to intensify the flavour of the meat and to tenderize the flesh.

The same is true as regards the hanging of birds and, although this process is most commonly used for game birds and wild waterfowl, the process can also be utilized to great effect to increase the flavour and tenderize the meat of domestically reared species such as duck, geese and guinea fowl. The hanging times in this chapter offer a minimum and maximum hanging time for each species, but it is down to your particular palate how long you hang your birds for; the longer they hang, the stronger they become, and a very well hung bird may be far too rich and gamey for your taste.

In the past pheasant used to be hung by the neck and the bird was not considered ready to cook until the flesh around the neck had rotted and, as a result, the body had fallen to the floor. This process produced a bird so strong in flavour that few today would find it palatable; especially those used to the insipid meat of commercially produced birds. Hanging produces a much more earthy flavour; if you have never eaten hung birds before then start out with the minimum hanging time and work your way up to the maximum hanging time to find the period that best suits your particular taste.

It is one of the great beauties of home butchering that you can carry out a bespoke process that best suits the needs of you and your family. If you are concerned about the hanging process leading to the decomposition of the bird and the build up of bacteria then do not be; although the hanging bird is in a process of decay and there is a build of bacteria, this should not present a health issue if the bird is correctly processed and cooked.

The home-produced hung bird if correctly handled is no more dangerous than a chicken bought from the supermarket; in fact the home butchered bird, whether domestically reared or taken from the wild, is probably healthier than a bought bird because the bought bird, unless it is organic, will have been reared with the use of drugs, including antibiotics, which leave a residue in the bird's flesh. Commercially butchered birds also go through a process where the flesh is pumped with water to increase the weight of the carcase, altering both the texture and the flavour of the meat. These are artificial processes that produce artificial meat; hanging on the other hand is entirely natural and is not a process that should concern you.

Any bacteria present in the carcase will be destroyed if the bird is correctly cooked. Birds, like small game, must be hung in a cool and airy place to which flies have no access or you will soon have a bird that is alive with maggots, which is not a pleasant sight and is a waste of a bird. As a home butcher I believe we have a moral responsibility to ensure that every conceivable part of the bird or small game is used, with nothing going to waste, especially in a world where hunger blights such a huge number of people.

The age of the bird has an influence on the amount of time that it needs to hang: young birds are very tender and possess a delicate flavour that is lost if over-hung, whereas older birds have tough flesh that needs to hang for longer in order for it to be tenderized. An old bird used too quickly will produce meat like boot leather – tough and chewy – so getting the hanging period right has a direct impact on the quality of the meal that will be produced.

As a home butcher you have to master the art of hanging and, in order to do this, you must be able to identify the age of the birds that you are dealing with. A game bird does not come with identification discs that give you the bird's age: you must calculate the age using a knowledge of the bird's anatomy to identify what stage of life it is at. We are not talking about ageing the bird to the very day of its birth; we simply need to know if it is a bird in the first session, under a year old, or whether it is an older bird of two or more years.

Ageing birds is not relevant to the smallholder's domestically reared poultry or waterfowl: you will know how old these birds are and so ageing a bird by its anatomical features relates only to birds taken from the wild. For the smallholder the most common bird in this category is the pheasant. The male pheasant, like a domestically reared cockerel, has spurs on the inside of its legs; these look like a claw and there is one on each leg below the feather line. As the pheasant ages these spurs alter, so they can be used to give a fairly accurate indication as to the bird's age.

On young cock birds, the spur will be short and have a rounded end, on two-year-old birds the spur will have increased in size and be in possession of a point, while on older birds the spur is thick, much longer and develops a vicious, sharp point. Hen pheasants do not have spurs so they are aged by the underside of the feet. On a young bird the feet will be soft, pliable and clean but on older birds the feet will be hard and rough. Another way to age a bird, either male or female, is to feel the breastbone: on young birds the breastbone is soft and pliable but on older birds the breastbone is hard.

Pheasant accounts for roughly eighty-five per cent of the national bag of game birds, so it is the pheasant that you are most likely to deal with. Due to the large number of pheasant available they can still be purchased quite cheaply from a game dealer, or to acquire a brace of free pheasant you can always offer your services as a beater to a local shoot. It is also worth considering joining a local syndicate on a DIY shoot, as this will afford you good shooting and provide you with pheasant throughout the session, with some left over to go in the freezer.

Another game bird that you might encounter is the partridge. There are two main species of partridge in this country: the grey partridge and the red-legged partridge. The legs of the grey partridge are used as a tool to age the bird: immature birds in their first session have yellowish legs and dark beaks, whereas mature birds sport grey legs and a pale beak. The plumage of the red-legged partridge is used to determine age – principally by examining the flight feathers. Rather than me trying to explain the location of these feathers simply refer to the diagram below which illustrates the topography of the bird.

With red-legged partridge in their first session an examination of the two outermost flight feathers will reveal that they have creamy tips, a marking that is not present on older birds. Red grouse are also aged by means of their outer flight feathers, although with the grouse you are looking at the shape of these feathers and not the markings. On young grouse the two outermost flight feathers will be pointed, whereas on a mature bird these flight feathers will be rounded at the end. When ageing waterfowl it comes down to the colour of the feet and bill: the feet and bill of the younger bird will be paler than those of a mature bird.

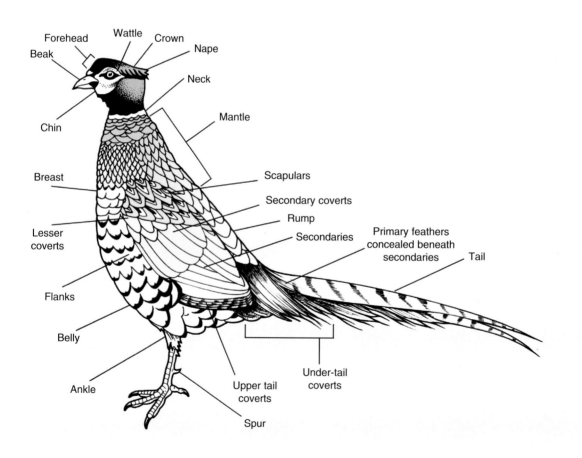

Topography of the bird.

Primaries

The primary feathers.

Now that the approximate age of the bird has been established it is time to turn our attention to the hanging time: remember that the older the bird the longer it has to hang. Let us begin with domestically reared birds – poultry or waterfowl – raised on your holding. Today the practice is not to hang domestically reared birds but to process them right away; plucking taking place immediately after slaughter and drawing following straight on after that.

However, this has not always been the case. In the past the smallholder would not consider it proper to proceed with such haste, believing that the bird would not be tender or flavoursome enough without being hung.

DIFFERENCE BETWEEN ADULT AND IMMATURE WATERFOWL

Bird	Adult	Immature
Pink-footed goose	Pink legs and feet, small dark head, dark neck, bill black and pink, colour pale blue-grey	Paler legs, browner in colour, paler on neck
White-fronted goose	Pink bill with white patch at base, orange legs, broad irregular black bars on belly, colour grey	No pink bill, or white patch at base of bill, or black blotches on the belly
Grey leg goose	Orange-yellow bill, pink legs and feet, colour pale grey	Legs a greyish pink
Canada goose	Black neck, light chest, white throat patch, black legs, black bill	No obvious difference
Mallard	Male: green head, orange bill, white neck ring, purplish brown breast Female: some orange on bill, mottled brown body	No obvious difference
Teal	Male: horizontal white stripe over ring, dark chestnut head Female: speckled brown and buff	No obvious difference
Wigeon	Male: chestnut head with yellow forehead Female: short blue-grey bill	No obvious difference

These smallholders were dealing with birds that matured more slowly and that lived considerably longer before they were slaughtered. Today cockerels and ducks are killed between nine to fourteen weeks of age, so it is not considered necessary to tenderize the meat by hanging. However, the hanging process has another function and that is to develop the flavour of the meat; modern poultry and duck meat, even when raised on a smallholding, lacks flavour and so the hanging of domestically reared birds is of benefit.

A professional slaughterman and butcher in Wales once told me that the flavour of the meat was entirely dependant on the correct hanging of a carcase, whether it was a bird or a beef cow: if you do not hang for long enough (or worse do not hang at all) then the flavour of the meat suffers. So I am a firm believer in the hanging of all meat. With chickens raised for the table, depending on the size of the bird, one or two days is sufficient, while with an older laying bird you could extend to three days. However, all of this is dependant on the weather: in winter you can obviously hang for longer, but in the height of summer the heat will only allow a day for hanging, unless you have a cool larder or cold room.

Ducks can be hung for one day, but for geese two or three days would be more appropriate. A wild goose can be hung for up to twenty-one days, but this would be far too long for a domestically reared goose and would damage rather than enhance the flavour.

Some smallholders keep guinea fowl or quail, both of which are game birds from the same family as the pheasant and the partridge (the Phasianidae family). The guinea fowl has a slaughter weight of 1½lb (700g) to 2½lb (1kg) at the age of roughly ten weeks and the quail a slaughter weight of ½lb at just six weeks old. Remembering the principle that hanging times are based on the size and age of the bird, the quail will require just a single day of hanging and the guinea fowl, which is approximately the same weight as a pheasant, will require three days.

Some smallholders keep turkeys in small numbers for the Christmas period. The turkey, which is a very large bird that can have a slaughter weight of around 30lb (13kg) reached at twenty-four weeks, can hang for eight days. This was Mrs Beeton's preferred time for the hanging of turkey, the time being reduced to five days during warmer weather.

Let us now move onto wild game birds and waterfowl. Pheasant should hang for between three to ten days, depending on your particular preference and the age of the bird; I prefer a bird that has hung for the full ten days but most people seem to have a palate suited to a bird that has hung for five to seven days. Grouse requires two to seven days and partridge two to eight days. Ducks, whatever the species, require just one or two days but geese will need to hang for between ten and twenty-one days (twenty-one days is required for the older, larger geese).

Let us now turn our attention to the pigeon – both feral and wood – which are both classed as vermin and are readily available in most parts of the country. Farmers are more than willing to let you onto their land to shoot either species, which appear in large flocks, allowing the shooter to take healthy bags (sometimes in the hundreds) on each outing. The pigeon is therefore a cheap source of high quality meat and all you have to do to take advantage of this bounty is learn to use a gun.

Although this is a book on butchering, I think that it is worth considering the subject of the feral pigeon in a bit more detail because they offer an excellent source of meat that is totally overlooked, unlike the wood pigeon, which everybody recognizes as a valuable food source. However, I shall just finish off the subject of hanging before we go any further on the feral pigeon.

Pigeons should not hang at all: they should be processed at the earliest opportunity and drawn as soon as possible after shooting. Some of the old-time shooters used to carry a hook or bent nail, with which they would draw the intestines whilst still in the field. If left hanging with the intestines in place, the pigeon will spoil and become unpleasant eating. Mrs Beeton says that the pigeon also requires a great deal of washing in order to get the best flavour from the meat, however, today top chefs believe that the washing of the bird removes flavour; personally I go with Mrs Beeton's approach.

Just because the pigeon should not hang, it does not mean that it has to be eaten straight away; once the bird is plucked, drawn and cleaned it can go in the fridge for a couple of days until required. Obviously, if you have shot hundreds of pigeons they will need to be stored in a freezer. A particular favourite among diners is squab pigeon, which is pigeon under the age of four months. The wood pigeon squab is recognized by the fact that it does not have the familiar white ring marking around its neck, displayed by all wood pigeons over the age of four months.

Unlike small game, a bird is always hung by a piece of string, tied around the neck, from which the bird may be suspended. While in some countries birds are hung by the feet – like small game – that has never been the practice in this country. As mentioned earlier, it is vital that the birds are hung in an environment that is free of flies; once the meat has incurred fly strike, also known as being flyblown, it is unsuitable for consumption. It is possible to purchase nets inside which the bird or small game can be hung. The mesh of these nets is so dense that flies cannot enter or strike through them; they are inexpensive and it is well worth having a couple in your butcher's kit to guard valuable meat.

The only other requirement for hanging is to make sure that each bird is hung separately and that there is a plentiful free flow of air around it. If you hang several birds together the heat that they can generate is quite incredible; such heat will lead to a rapid build up of bacteria so the birds must be kept as cool as possible. Heat is your adversary when hanging meat of any kind, which is why birds and small game were traditionally hung in cellars or stone sheds.

Feral Pigeon

I feel justified in mentioning the feral pigeon in this book because part of the home butcher's job is to seek out good quality meat that can be processed on the smallholding. Whilst everybody is aware of the merits of rabbit, chicken and pheasant for this purpose, very few smallholders and shooters are aware of the value of the feral pigeon.

The feral pigeon is the bird that you see in London's Trafalgar Square and in every other city centre up and down the country. These birds, which have a national population in the multiple millions, also appear in factories, railway stations, store sheds and on farms. They are considered a pest almost everywhere and are officially designated as vermin; land owners and factory owners are, therefore, only too happy to allow anyone with the ability to use a suitable rifle to remove these birds from their premises.

The origins of the feral pigeon stem from a time when dovecotes where a familiar site on farms and in villages. Huge dovecotes housed hundreds of pigeons, the birds were kept semi-feral and used as a valuable source of meat; pigeon pie being a regular dish on the country dweller's dining table. When farm-reared meat became more widely available, pigeon fell out of fashion and the pigeons in the dovecotes were no longer fed. The birds moved away from the dovecotes to seek out food and very rapidly established themselves right across the country, thriving around man in cities or in farmyards.

One of the main reasons why feral pigeon is so underused is because most shooters see it as a flying rat, which it most certainly is not. It does not, for example, spread such diseases as leptospirosis or murine typhus, both of which can be carried by rats and can kill people. The feral pigeon is not a carrion bird and does not feed on unpleasant items such as road kill, but in cities it feeds on the same food as man – bits of bread or other food that has been thrown away by people – which, in a city, accounts

A bag of feral pigeons taken from a local farm.

for tonnes of food every year. In the country the feral pigeon takes food from around farm buildings, exactly the same food that is given to cattle or the grain harvested for human consumption.

This assumption by many shooters that feral pigeons are feeding on a similar diet to rats is ridiculous; a shooter once told me that he would not touch feral pigeon because he believed that they fed on medical waste. Such statements simply display a lack of knowledge regarding the feeding habits of these birds. In fact, during the Second World War, the Ministry of Food encouraged the hunting of feral pigeon, citing that it was an excellent

source of nutrition at a time when rationing was in full force and meat was in very short supply. The feral pigeon is therefore a safe and valuable source of meat that can be taken by any smallholder with the ability to use an air rifle, affording them meat that costs nothing but the price of a pellet. If you can get access to feral pigeons I strongly advise you to do so, you will not regret it.

PLUCKING

Now that your bird has been correctly hung, it is time to turn your attention to removing the feathers: a process known as plucking, which entails pulling out the feathers without damaging the skin beneath. Many books will tell you that a chicken must be plucked straight away after killing because that is when the feathers will come out most easily; that is indeed the case, but it does not mean that the bird cannot be plucked at a later stage if required, after hanging for example.

As a chicken, or any bird for that matter, cools the skin contracts and the follicular cavities in which the base of the feathers are rooted become constricted, tightening their grip on the base of the feathers, making them more difficult to pull out, but certainly not impossible. Do not be concerned by those people who tell you that a chicken must be plucked straight after death, that may be the easiest time to pluck it, but it is not the only time, so if you want to hang your chicken for a day or two it can still be plucked at the end of the hanging process.

This may be an old-fashioned approach that is not commonly used today, but that does not mean that it is flawed approach; in fact, I find that many of the old ways of doing things on the smallholding are superior to the modern methods. With birds that have hung for a long time, such as pheasant or goose, you have to take care when plucking that you do not tear the skin, which becomes more fragile the longer the bird hangs. Tearing the skin leads to the flesh beneath drying out, simply due to contact with the atmosphere. In America, where game birds are often skinned in the field (the Americans having no taste for hung birds) the process is done very quickly and the bird is placed immediately in a plastic bag, which is then sealed because contact with the atmosphere rapidly dries it out.

If lumps of skin are torn away during the plucking process, when the bird is roasted these bare patches of flesh will dry out to such a degree that when eaten they will have the texture of wood. It is far better to pluck a bird slowly, without tearing the skin, than it is to pluck a bird quickly and have lumps of skin missing all over the place. The mark of a good butcher is not speed, but the quality of the prepared carcase.

When it comes to little birds, like quail, extreme care must be exercised when plucking, or you will simply tear all the skin off as you pluck, as it is so thin and delicate on such small birds. The person plucking the bird should be seated, wearing an apron and with a sack across their knees. There will be a lot of feathers, many of them airborne; as they have a tendency to stick to parts of the body where the most irritation will be incurred, like the end of the nose, it is therefore a good idea to have a clean towel handy so that you can remove irritating feathers from time to time.

The method that follows is for dry plucking: you will read about wet plucking in some books which involves the bird being dipped in water before plucking. This may work for some, but in my experience all it does is turn the feathers into the stickiest objects I have ever come across. They adhere to everything in sight, including your hands and face, and after a session of wet plucking I end up looking like some kind of birdman. Try wet plucking if you wish but be prepared for a lot of mess; I prefer to stick to the conventional dry plucking method.

Some people scald the bird with hot water before plucking, in the belief that this opens the follicular cavities in which the feathers are rooted and therefore makes the plucking process easier. I am not convinced that pouring hot water over the skin is a sound practice, for the simple reason that if you pour hot water over your own skin you will damage it, so surely the same happens to the skin of a bird when you pour hot water over it? Besides, all these measures to try to loosen the feathers prior to plucking are totally unnecessary in my opinion; it is not as though the feathers are rooted in concrete. They are not that difficult to pull out, apart from some of the smaller wing feathers which, I concede, are very tenacious.

1. Plucking should begin on the back. Take a few feathers between the finger and thumb and then with a sharp, downward pull tug them out; pull upward and you will risk damaging the skin. Do not try and take too many feathers at a time as this again will lead to you damaging the skin, just take a few at a time.
2. I'm not sure why you start on the back, but as that is the way that it has always tra-ditionally been done that is the method that I adhere to. When the back is plucked and the neck up to the base of the head, the bird is turned over and the breast is plucked in the same manner. The large tail feathers and the large wing feathers are next pulled out individually, followed by the rest of the wing feathers, which may come out several at a time. When you come to the very fine feathers along the

leading edge of the wing, which are very tenacious, you will find that they are best pulled out with a pair of pliers. Plucking is by no means a difficult undertaking, anybody can pluck a bird and do a good job as long as one basic rule is followed: take your time; the only thing that messes a bird up is rushing the job.

In the past, when birds were plucked by hand and not by machine, a professional working in a commercial operation could pluck a bird in five minutes. This is an astonishing achievement and something that you should not try to emulate; if you can get down to quarter of an hour you will be doing well, but for most beginners it will take a good half-hour or more to pluck a bird properly. Plucking machines are really only worth considering if you are running a commercial enterprise. They pluck a bird very

To pluck a bird you want to be seated, with an apron on and a sack across your knees. The bird is positioned across your knee, with its feet down and it breast against the knee.

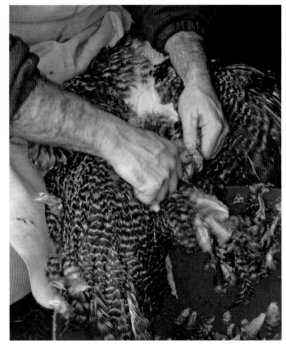

Plucking should begin on the back. Take a few feathers between your finger and thumb and give a sharp downward tug.

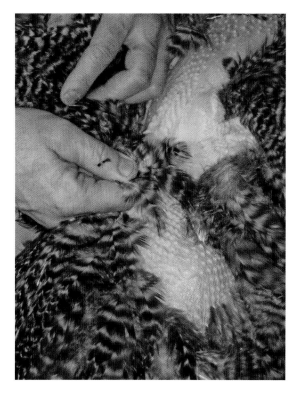

To make a successful job of plucking the feathers should be removed without damaging the skin; take a small handful at a time and pull downwards.

rapidly, but the main advantage of a machine, if you are doing a large number of birds, is that it is less tiring for the person who is plucking the birds.

For example, if you have fifty birds to pluck and you are able to get down to ten minutes per bird, it will still take you eight-and-a-half hours of hard work to pluck them; by which time you will have very tired hands and wrists and a stiff back. With a machine the same task should be reduced to about four-and-a- half hours, the reduced amount of time not only speeding up the operation, but also reducing the amount of physical stress placed on the person doing the plucking.

A plucking machine will cost roughly £300 and will soon pay for itself, due simply to the large amount of work-hours such a machine will save; so for any smallholding running a small poultry enterprise, the purchase of a plucking machine is well worthwhile. Plucking machines are very easy to use and most people soon get to grips with the technique; very experienced operators are able to do a staggering twenty birds per hour. A plucking machine is not specific to chickens and will pluck any bird you care to mention, from tiny quail right up to the biggest goose you can find.

After plucking most birds will have a few hairs on the carcase; ducks and geese, with their heavy under-down, have more than most and these need to be removed by singeing. Some books suggest using a propane torch for this purpose, but the flame of a propane torch is very powerful and unforgiving; if you do not handle it very carefully you will end up charring the skin of the bird, so I prefer to use a much gentler flame in the form of a candle. All that is required is to place the candle in a candleholder, light the wick and then hold the bird over the flame. Deal with each hair individually by lowering the bird towards the flame so that the hair comes into contact with the tip of the flame, only the end of the hair needs to contact the flame and it will disintegrate. Move from one hair to the next and you will soon have them all removed.

A simple plucking machine.

DRAWING AND DRESSING THE BIRD

Drawing refers to the removal of the bird's internal organs, which is necessary with nearly all birds, the odd exception being the woodcock.

1. The operation begins at the head end of the bird with the bird being placed on the workbench, breast up. The head is removed and then a long incision is made along the top of the neck, from a point at the base of the neck where it joins the body and running all the way up beneath the skin to the top of the neck.

2. Fold the skin back and detach it from the neck: you should be able to do this just by pulling and teasing with the hands but, if there does prove to a be a stubborn piece of skin, then use a knife to separate it from the neck.

3. Use a heavy knife to cut through the base of the neck below the bottom vertebra, then turn the bird over onto its back and you will see along the front of the neck a food sack, known as the crop, which needs to be removed with the neck. With birds that have been hanging, the contents of the crop may well have liquefied and so you need to take care when removing it so that none of the contents spill onto the bird's flesh.

4. This can be done with the bird's neck hanging down over the edge of a table when the crop is removed; any spillage will then run downwards away from the bird's flesh. Gentle palpation of the crop will reveal whether the contents are liquefied or not. Many books depict a method in which the neck of the bird is not plucked, but is simply left in feather and severed at the base of the neck with a cleaver. However, I consider this method to be wasteful as the neck of a bird can be used to make stock, soups and gravies, so it should be plucked and removed and used.

5. If you have removed the neck in its entirety you will now have a small hole in the bird's breast that goes between the clavicles (commonly know as the wishbone) that provides sufficient room for one or more fingers to be inserted, depending on the size of your fingers. Place one or two fingers inside the chest cavity of the bird and move them around using a circular motion to loosen the lungs and other organs from their attachments. If you have cut the skin away from the neck correctly, you will now have a fold of skin that can be brought up to seal the hole in the chest, the flap reaching generously down the bird's breast.

6. Now turn your attention to the other end of the bird, lifting the parson's nose and making a careful incision in a direct line from the centre of the parson's nose to the vent. Through this incision you will be able to see the intestine: put your finger in through the incision and push the intestine gently backward, away from the vent and then make a circular incision around the vent.

7. Now take the vent with your finger and thumb and pull gently and you will see the intestine drawn out; do not pull too hard or you will pull the intestine away from the rest of the internal organs. When the intestines are drawn, reach in past them and take hold of the gizzard and pull firmly. At this point, if you have loosened the lungs correctly, all of the internal organs will be drawn out with the gizzard. Wipe round the inside of the bird with a damp cloth and the drawing process is complete.

It must be remembered with birds that have been hanging for a considerable time that the internal organs are in a fragile state, the drawing must therefore be carried out with care so as not to rupture the intestine, which will cause a spillage of intestinal juices or faeces. If this does happen it can be cleaned with plenty of cold water, but it is far better to avoid a

The drawing process begins at the head end of the bird, with the bird breast up on the workbench. The head should be removed prior to commencing this operation. Make an incision in the skin of the neck, running from the base of the neck to the top of the neck. Free the skin from the neck and then, using a strong knife, cut through the neck below the bottom-most vertebra.

BELOW: You will see attached to the front of the neck a food sack (left), known as the crop, which must be removed intact with the neck (right), then removed from the neck and discarded.

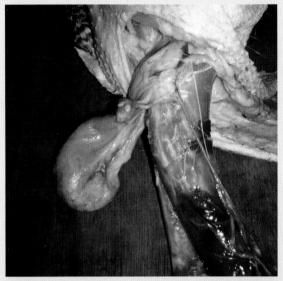

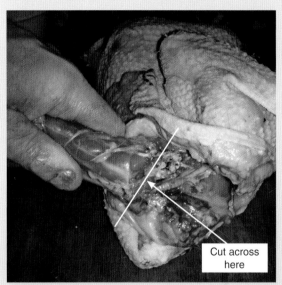

Cut across here

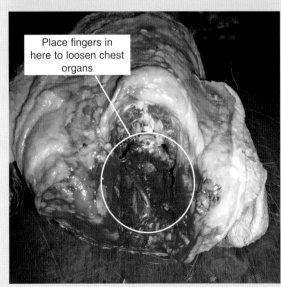

Place fingers in here to loosen chest organs

Now insert your finger into the hole in the chest and loosen the lungs and other organs from their attachments; fold the neck skin flap up and over the hole in the chest and then fold the flap across the upper chest.

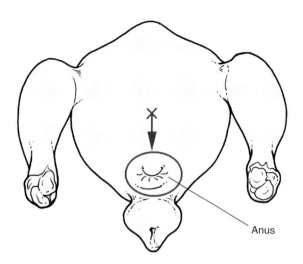

To open the rear of the carcase so that the internal organs may be drawn out make an incision from the mark × in the direction of the parson's nose, cutting down to the point marked by the arrow, then make a complete circular cut around the anus.

Anus

rupture in the intestine or bowels during the drawing process. If you pull on the gizzard and all that comes away is the gizzard without being followed by the other internal organs, you haven't loosened them correctly from the hole in the breast. If this does happen then fold down the flap at the front of the bird, insert a finger and correctly loosen the organs, then go to the other end of the bird, reach in and draw out the remaining organs.

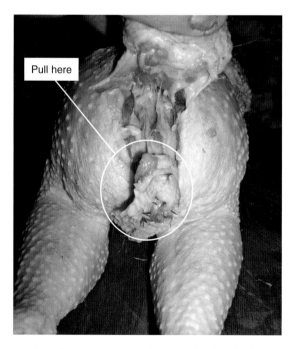

Pull here

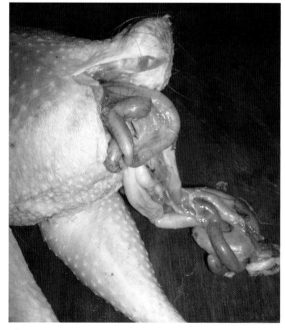

Take hold of the vent between the finger and thumb and pull gently; when the intestines are drawn out reach down and past them to take hold of the gizzard. Pull on the gizzard firmly and you will be able to withdraw all the internal organs in one go.

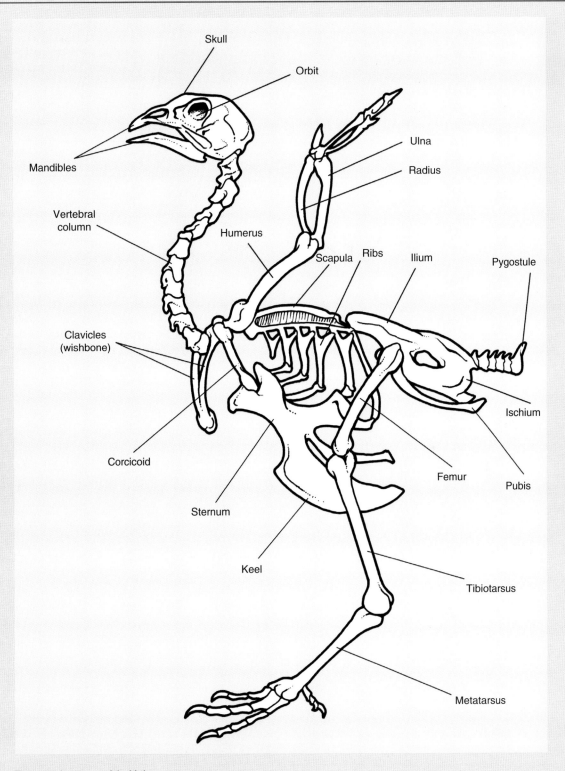

Skull

Orbit

Ulna

Radius

Mandibles

Vertebral
column

Humerus

Scapula   Ribs   Ilium   Pygostule

Clavicles
(wishbone)

Ischium

Corcicoid

Femur   Pubis

Sternum

Keel

Tibiotarsus

Metatarsus

The internal structure of the bird.

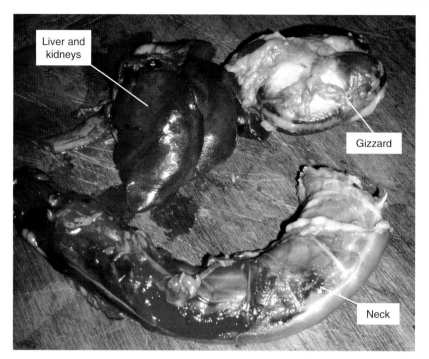

The liver, kidneys, neck and gizzard are collectively known as the giblets and should be passed to the kitchen where the cook can make good use of them.

If you examine the parson's nose you will find a small rise at the front of it: this is the oil gland, which is used by the bird when preening to apply the oil from the gland to its feathers to keep them waterproof and supple. This oil gland is removed by simply making a cut beneath it.

Along the front edge of the wings where the ulna and radius meet at a joint, there is a point resembling a claw, and on the furthermost tip of the wing there is another point; both of these are removed with a knife, simply because they are pointed in nature and could cause an injury to a diner.

It is worth considering for a moment the modern fashion for cutting the wings of game birds off with a cleaver, at the joint where they join the body. The reasoning is that there is very little meat on the wings so why bother plucking them? In my opinion this is a wasteful approach: firstly the wing may not carry a large amount of meat but it does carry some and it should not be wasted, simply in order to save the five or ten

minutes required to pluck the wings. Secondly the primary feathers – the large wing feathers from game birds, especially the male pheasant – are stunning and make fine decorations stuck in the brim of a hat or placed in a vase with some dried flowers. Simply throwing these feathers away to avoid spending a few minutes plucking them is a waste. I also think that the carcase of a bird looks more professionally finished if the wings have been plucked rather than cut off.

There is another technique called breasting: this involves the breast of small birds like partridge or pigeon being plucked, then the skin being opened and the breast meat removed. This operation can be carried out in a couple of minutes and the rest of the bird is then thrown away. The argument is that the greater portion of the meat on a small bird is in the breast so, rather than plucking the entire bird, why not just remove the breast and ignore the rest of the bird? You will not find the breasting technique taught in this book because I find it abhorrent

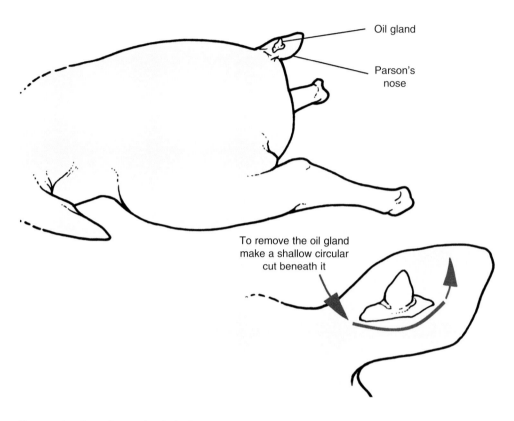

Oil gland

Parson's nose

To remove the oil gland make a shallow circular cut beneath it

The procedure for cutting out the oil gland.

that the greater portion of the bird is simply thrown away and only the breasts are used.

When it comes to the pig, most smallholders are familiar with the phrase that: 'Everything can be used but the squeak', which is perfectly true. The head can be turned into brawn, the trotters roasted or barbecued, the skin turned into suede; even the intestines can be used to make the casing for sausages. The smallholder should take the same approach to the use of birds, even small ones like pigeon: every single scrap of meat that can be recovered should be used. I consider this to be not only a moral obligation but also a financial one: taking the trouble to recover every last scrap of meat from the animals that come to our butcher's

bench saves a lot of money, which is of great importance in these times of austerity.

The bird is now almost ready for the oven but it still has its feet on. In Mrs Beeton's time, birds like duck and goose were actually cooked and served with the feet still attached, along with the head, which was fully plucked. Today people would find such a presentation off-putting and so the feet are removed. To remove the feet make a circular cut through the skin and down to the bone, around the joint where the tibiotarsus and metatarsus meet, then place this joint on the edge of a table and push down on the lower leg. The joint will snap apart and, as you pull the lower leg away from the upper leg, you will see the leg tendons that

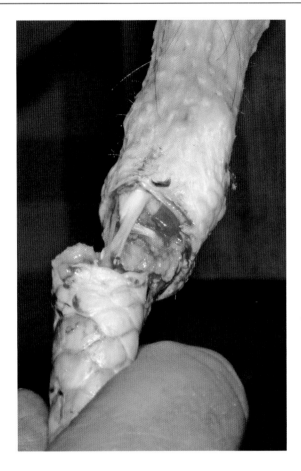

To remove the foot of a bird, cut through the skin of the hock joint down to the bone. Place the joint on the edge of a table and push down on the lower leg; the joint will snap open and you will see the leg tendons.

attach the lower leg to the muscles in the upper leg; do not cut through these tendons, but pull very firmly on the lower leg and you will pull the tendons away from their anchor points in the muscle. Once detached the tendons will be drawn away by continuing to pull on the lower leg.

The reason that the tendons are removed is simply because they are very unpleasant to eat: they have the consistency of a rubber band and if eaten they are difficult to digest. Many people simply cut the lower leg of game birds off at the hock joint with one blow from a cleaver, thus leaving the tendons in place. They then have to be removed on the plate before someone eats them. As home butchers we are required to remove the foot and lower leg, I therefore see no reason why we should not also remove the leg tendons from game birds, as we do for small game, in order to present the diner with a better presented bird.

Pull firmly on the lower leg and the tendons will be wrenched from their anchor points and drawn from the upper leg.

TO WASH OR NOT TO WASH

Some books tell you to wash a bird's carcase when the drawing and dressing process is completed, whilst others tell you that to wash the bird is to take away the flavour; personally I think that the washing of the bird does not diminish the flavour and is a worthwhile exercise. The washing removes bodily fluids, dirt and small feathers. Holding the bird under a running tap, so that the water runs through the bird's body cavity is quick and easy. When it comes to shot birds the tap sometimes dislodges bits of loose shot from inside the bird that if not removed could easily be dislodged if the bird were to be stuffed. There are many recipes for the stuffing of game birds and wild fowl and the loose shot can become mixed with the stuffing if not removed.

The washing of birds whether domestically reared or taken from the wild is therefore a valuable exercise. Once you have washed the body cavity examine it carefully to see that all the internal organs have been removed, including the kidneys, which are located high up against the back, just outside the ribcage and the sexual organs, which are located in the rump end of the bird and are attached very firmly. Once you are thoroughly satisfied that the internal organs have been fully removed and the bird's body cavity has been well washed, move on to wash the outside of the bird. Dry the bird thoroughly inside and out with a clean tea towel and place it on a wire rack – the one found in the grill pan of an oven will do nicely – and leave the bird to finish drying naturally.

REMOVING SHOT

Birds taken from the wild are obviously shot, usually with a shotgun, which fires numerous pieces of shot from a cartridge, spreading out a fan of projectiles, many of which will have hit the target bird. Every effort must be made by the home butcher to remove all the shot, or the diner will end up with a very hard piece of metal

in their mouth, which, if bitten down upon, could crack a tooth. Once a bird is plucked it is quite obvious from an examination of the carcase where the shot entered the body of the bird; the blood vessels at the point of entry will have been severed, releasing blood into the surrounding flesh, causing a reddening of the flesh, which resembles a very small bruise.

Most of the shot will have passed through the flesh, as it needs to strike the vital organs in order to cause death. However, some shot may well remain in the flesh parts of the bird and these pieces of shot must be removed using tweezers if the shot is visible; if it is not visible probe the wound with a cocktail stick or large needle to try and tease the shot out like a surgeon. You can buy small magnetic devices that can be used to locate the shot but I don't think these are really necessary; no shot can enter a bird without leaving its mark. If you study the carcase of the bird carefully you will see the evidence of shot entering the body and be able to ascertain if the shot stopped in the flesh, or continued into the organs to inflict a mortal wound.

You must also examine the inside of the bird for shot, not just the outside. Shot is made up of small ball bearings that are smooth, rather

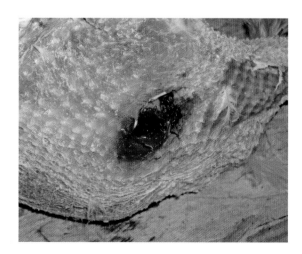

The entry of shot can be seen by the deep red marking of the flesh, which results from the rupturing of the blood vessels.

than sharp shrapnel, so if a piece of shot is missed and accidentally swallowed, it will not lacerate the intestine but will simply be passed with other waste material without causing any damage. Some birds, such as pigeon, are shot using an air weapon. Airguns do not use a cartridge full of shot, instead they fire a single projectile in the form of a pellet, which is generally placed in the head of the bird so the flesh is totally unmarked and there is no shot to hunt down.

TRUSSING

Trussing is a method of restraining the wings and legs of the bird in a certain position, so that they do not move during the cooking process; this apparently prevents the bird from drying out during cooking. However, today many cooks do not bother trussing a bird, preferring to use tin foil to prevent the bird from drying out in the oven. As a home butcher you should, however, know how to truss a bird should the need arise to carry out this operation, as it will, for example, if the bird is going to be frozen. The frozen bird is trussed so that it not only keeps its shape but also takes up as little space as possible in the freezer.

There are some very complex methods of trussing a bird using thread and long needles, but these are unnecessary and difficult to master. All that is required to truss a bird is some parcel string; do not use hemp string as it has a hairy surface and you will end up with fine hairs from the string on the meat of the bird. Place the bird on its back and simply tie a length of string to the base of the parson's nose with the knot facing you, then run one end of the string around one leg and the other length of string around the other leg. Cross the two lengths of string under the back of the parson's nose, bring the two lengths together over the knot that you have already tied and then tie a second knot to secure the legs to the side of the parson's nose.

This sounds very complicated but, as you will see from the diagram, it is very simple. Some people now run the string over the leg, cross it halfway up the back and then run it around the bird, to secure the wings to the side of the body and hold the neck flap down. However, I simply take another length of string and run it twice around the chest end of the bird, securing the wings to the side of the bird and holding the neck flap firmly in place. This method is not only a more simple approach; it is also more practical if the bird is to be stuffed. The cook only needs to cut the string at the rear of the bird, stuff it and then retie, but if the same length of string had been used to secure both ends of the bird, the cook will have to retie both ends; as my method saves time and effort in the kitchen it is always appreciated.

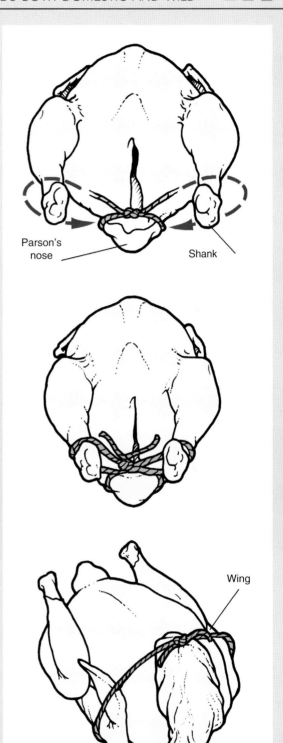

Tie the string to the base of the parson's nose then pass the ends of the string under the shanks.

Once the string is under the shanks pull them to the side of the parson's nose then return the string back to the base of the parson's nose and tie a knot.

Simply pass a length of string around the chest that captures the wings and the top of the skin flap then tie tightly.

The process of trussing a bird. The same method is used no matter what the type of bird.

SMALL BIRD BUTCHERING

When it comes to very small birds, like pigeon and quail, there are a few differences in the preparation of the bird, which I shall now highlight, but in all other respects the processing of the small bird is exactly the same as the method outlined above. Although I have stated that the wings of a bird should be plucked and the meat on them used, when it comes to small birds like quail and pigeon, the amount of meat on the wing is so minuscule that it is not worth plucking them and so I remove the wings, head and feet of small birds, using a pair of shears, before I start the plucking process. The wing should be cut off at the end of the humerus, just behind the ball joint.

Remove the head.

Remove the wings.

Remove the feet.

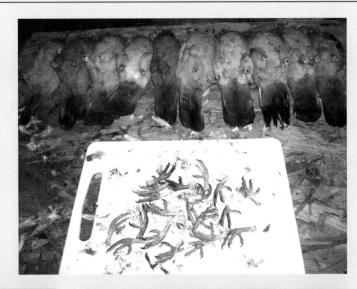

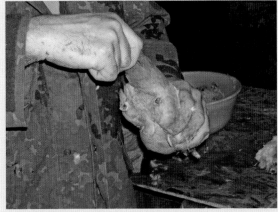

Remove the tail feathers.

Pluck and dress as with other birds.

chapter six

THE PRESERVATION OF MEAT

INTRODUCTION

Personally I prefer to take meat in season: harvesting rabbits in late autumn and throughout the winter, taking pigeon during the rest of the year and when poultry is slaughtered on the holding, I take it as and when required. This means that I do not need to use a freezer to preserve my meat, as it comes to me fresh.

However, plenty of smallholders do use a freezer and this is quite understandable if your small game or game birds are taken in large numbers. For example, if you have ten pheasant you cannot hang them and then consume them before the meat spoils, so you need some form of storage. Some hunters when they go lamping for rabbits will have been called in by a farmer to carry out a pest control operation; they have to make a large impact on the rabbit population and this can mean taking forty to ninety rabbits in a single outing. Once again these could not be consumed before the meat spoiled.

I go to my rabbiting grounds, take what is required for the planned meal and then return home, only going back into the field the next time we require meat for a meal. In this way no storage is required, but not everyone has this luxury and so the freezer is not merely desirable, but an essential item to ensure the preservation of the meat. What kind of freezer – either chest or upright – boils down to personal taste: any modern freezer will do the

job to a very high standard and can be totally relied upon.

Although I do not use a freezer at the moment, I used to use one when it was legal to slaughter lambs on the holding. The meat could not all be consumed before it spoiled and so I stored the lambs in a large chest freezer, simply because it was large enough to take them. This is the best way to approach the subject of freezer selection: simply calculate your needs by working out roughly the number of rabbits and birds that you need to store and then purchasing a freezer that will hold that number. Allow a bit of extra capacity because you always seem to end up with more meat than you calculated for.

PREPARING MEAT FOR THE FREEZER

Hanging Before Freezing

Let us begin with the subject of hanging and the question: Should meat be hung before it goes into the freezer? The answer is yes, as it cannot be hung after it has been frozen. So, for example, if you intend to freeze a pheasant you would first hang it for the required amount of time to suit you palate and then you would pluck, draw, clean and truss the bird before it went into the freezer. The same approach should be used for small game, for example, a rabbit should be hung for a day and then be skinned, cleaned and trussed before being frozen.

Freezing Small Game and Birds Intact

You can freeze a bird in feather or a rabbit in fur: for example, you could place a pheasant in the freezer at the end of the hanging period, without plucking or drawing it. However, I do not think this a very good approach for various reasons: firstly, when the bird or small game thaws it will have damp fur or feathers. Plucking or skinning, which has to be done as quickly as possible once the bird or small game has thawed, is made more difficult because the skin, having been frozen, adheres tightly to the fur or feathers, making the skinning or plucking process a bit of a battle. Besides this, I am also not at all convinced that freezing a bird with its intestines in place is a good idea.

The biggest drawback to freezing birds or small game intact is that when you come to get the bird or rabbit from the freezer it is not ready for use: once thawed it still has to be processed. The final point to make about birds or small game that have been frozen intact is that they do not keep as long as those that have been fully processed.

A hare that has been frozen intact, for example, will have all its internal organs and intestines still in place and will still be wearing its skin. There are some quite heavy fat deposits between the flesh and the skin, as well as large fat deposits along the loin and around the kidneys. The fat deposits and the internal organs both break down in the freezer much more rapidly than flesh and bone; if they are removed and the carcase is frozen, it will last longer in the freezer than an intact rabbit or bird, due to the absence of fat and internal organs. The difference in storage times is several months: a hare carcase, for example, will store in a freezer for about eight moths, whereas a hare frozen intact will last only six months or even less.

Preparing a Carcase for Wrapping

Meat kept in a freezer can be stored whole or jointed but I think that the best option is to store whole carcasees, for the simple reason that a whole carcase has a considerably longer storage time than joints; for example, a pheasant carcase will last for eight months in the freezer, but if you joint that pheasant it will only last six months.

Obviously, if you store a bird or small game whole, you can use it for dishes that require the whole carcase and it gives you that additional level of flexibility, whereas meat stored in joints can only be used for dishes that require joints. Whilst some may argue that the small game or bird jointed takes up less space in the freezer, you are talking about a very small space saving; for example, a rabbit when jointed and packed takes up more or less the same amount of space in a freezer as a rabbit that is left whole.

To prepare a carcase for freezing, whether it is a bird or small game, you first want to truss it, as explained in the previous chapter. This has the effect of compressing the carcase into the most compact form possible. Next the end of the legs and wings should be examined, if they are pointed in any way they might pierce the plastic wrapping applied to the carcase for freezing; pointed wing or leg tips should, therefore, be covered by a sheath made out of several layers of tin foil. If the plastic wrapping is pierced, freezer gases will enter at the point of the piercing and burn the meat, destroying its flavour and so covering pointed wing tips or legs is time well spent.

Birds and small game should be dry and cool before they are wrapped: do not place a carcase in the freezer that still retains some body heat. You must also check the inside of the body cavity to ensure that all the fat deposits have been fully removed. These will break down more rapidly than meat and bone and if the bird or small game is left in the freezer for the full length of its storage time, any fat still present in the body cavity will break down and contaminate the meat.

Correct Wrapping

You can spend a lot of time butchering your small game or birds to a very high standard, having first hung them to perfection to produce a carcase that has excellent flavour. However, if you then make a poor job of freezing the meat you can destroy its taste. There is no great art or skill to the correct wrapping of small game or birds, all that is required is to wrap the meat in such a way that the freezer gases cannot come into contact with it. If this occurs the meat will suffer a form of burn known as freezer burn, which dries out the meat, altering the texture and destroying the flavour. To prevent this from happening the meat must be wrapped, firstly in freezer wrap, or in a heavy-duty plastic freezer bag and then in paper that is held in place using masking tape.

Placing two layers of covering over the meat may sound excessive, but many top American game hunters, who write about their exploits in books and magazines, advocate the double-wrapping of meat because their experiments over many years demonstrate that this method is markedly more effective at protecting the meat from the effects of freezer burn than single-wrapping. They also claim that the flavour of double-wrapped meat is superior to that of meat that has been single-wrapped.

I have to agree with these eminent hunters. When wrapping the meat in plastic freezer wrap, or when placing it in a freezer bag, it is important that you work hard to expel all the air from the bag or wrap, as any air left around the meat will freeze and cause a burn to the meat. The freezer gas that causes burn to the meat is the air that is present in a freezer, the object is therefore to protect the meat from coming into contact with this air. However, if air is left in a freezer bag or under freezer wrap, then the plastic covering is not providing a protective layer for the meat and is actually making things worse by trapping the air next to it.

If you want to be really professional, you can vacuum pack your meat. This involves using a device to extract all the air from the freezer bag,

which will ensure that the meat isn't burnt by any air left inside the bag. A small vacuum packing machine will cost somewhere in the region of £200, which is a viable proposition for someone running a business that involves the freezing of meat. However, for the home butcher whose objective is to save money, such a machine is not really a cost-effective purchase.

There are, however, some hand-operated devices on the market that draw the air from specially designed, and very durable, reusable vacuum pack freezer bags. These can be washed and reused over and over again, which not only makes good monetary sense, but it also has a positive effect on your carbon footprint, which is a concern for most smallholders. The manual zip-up vacuum packs go under the brand name ZipVac and can be purchased from a company called BushWear.

The manually operated zip-up vacuum packs cost around £10 and are probably the best way for the home butcher to provide an effective plastic covering for the meat they are preparing to freeze. Once your meat is securely encased in a protective plastic covering of some kind, you should then apply a paper wrapping, several layers in depth. For this purpose you require freezer paper, which has a shiny side and a dull side; it is the shiny side that goes against the meat. Wrap the meat securely in the freezer paper and then apply pressure with the hand to expel as much air as possible from the package; finally fold over the ends and tape the package up securely with ordinary masking tape. Every package must be labelled with a thick marker pen, with the date the package went into the freezer and the contents. In the case of birds, this should also include the age of the bird; there is nothing worse than retrieving a bird from the freezer for the purpose of roasting, for which you require a young bird, only to discover that you have retrieved an old bird only fit for soups and casseroles.

As regards game or birds that have hung, you should also note on the package the hanging period. When a bird that you have reared is packaged do not simply write chicken or duck, but write down the actual breed of the bird. Clearly marking the packages in this way will help you to select the exact item from the freezer that you require, for the meal that you are preparing. Next to the freezer you should keep a small notebook that has an entry for every package that went into it; you can then quickly ascertain what is available from cold storage. Do not forget to cross out items when they are removed from the freezer or you will be planning meals using meat that you have already cooked.

Storage Times

Meat stored in a freezer will not last for ever and when it comes to small game and birds it

MAXIMUM PERIOD OF FREEZER STORAGE		
Species	Whole carcase	Joints
Chicken	12 months	6 months
Duck	6–8 months	4–6 months
Turkey	6 months	4 months
Goose	6 months	4 months
Partridge	8 months	6 months
Grouse	8 months	6 months
Quail	8 months	6 months
Pheasant	8 months	6 months
Pigeon	4 months	3 months
Rabbit	6 months	6 months
Hare	8 months	6 months

will not even store for an entire year. This fact must be taken into account as you build up your freezer larder. For example, if you use two or three rabbits each week, this adds up to 104 to 156 rabbits per year. Rabbits last for only six months in the freezer so, if you take 90 to 100 rabbits in one week and store them all in the freezer, anywhere between twelve and forty rabbits will not be used because they will reach the end of their maximum storage time before you are able to consume them.

You therefore need to stagger the preservation of meat in your freezer to correlate with your specific requirements. So, for example, if you use four rabbits a week, which is a yearly requirement of 208 and, like me, you hunt rabbits for just six months of the year, take roughly thirty-five rabbits each month for freezer storage. Some hunters like to have just three or four big night shoots during the winter to harvest their yearly requirements, in which case you should go out every two months and bag roughly sixty-eight rabbits at a time.

As you can see you need to plan with great care what goes into your freezer and when, as it will not last for ever. If you do not pre-plan the storage of meat to align with your specific requirements, then meat will almost certainly go to waste.

Canning Meat

Meat can be preserved by home canning, a method that was used extensively before the invention of the freezer. However, canning is a very difficult process to get just right; if you happen to make a mistake the canned meat will develop botulism, which is a very dangerous form of food poisoning that can kill people. Canning of meat is therefore best left alone, as there is no indication that the meat is contaminated until you eat it. Besides which, canning requires the use of pressure cooking equipment and expensive jars, so you are far better off spending that money on a decent freezer, which is infinitely safer and easier to use for the storing of meat.

chapter seven

The Curing of Skins

INTRODUCTION

The skilled home butcher wastes nothing, finding a use for every usable part of the animals and birds that come across the butcher's bench; this includes using feathers and fur, both of which are normally thrown away, which is a waste of valuable resources. The indigenous peoples of the world, such as the Eskimo and the North American Indian, wasted nothing. Even animal bone was used to make tools: the small fine bones were used to make needles, the tendons of larger animals were extracted and used to make thread and the fur was used to make warm clothing, blankets and bags. The feathers were also used by the American Indian for decoration and to denote station, as demonstrated by the tribe chief's headdress – a thing of great beauty and grandeur.

We can also use the fur and feathers from the animals that we butcher, rather than throwing these natural resources away. The fur from rabbits used to be sent to London where it was turned into felt for the construction of bowler hats. This was a huge industry that employed many people, but the bowler hat fell out of fashion and modern fabrics are now used for everything so rabbit fur, which is rich and luxurious to wear, is simply thrown away.

Many people think that the curing of skins is a complex undertaking that requires all kinds of tools, knowledge and special chemicals. Whilst this may be true of commercially produced leather and pig skin pelts, it is not the case with much smaller rabbit or hare skins, which can be cured easily with no specialist equipment whatsoever. Fur clothing may not be in fashion,

but the items of clothing that I make from fur are taken from animals that have been killed for their meat; the fur is a by-product of that process and would be thrown away if I did not make use of it. I therefore do not see the wearing of this kind of fur as morally wrong – quite the opposite in fact – I see it as an environmentally sound and completely ethical practice that keeps alive the ancient skills used by our ancestors.

If you have never worn a fur garment I can tell you that the feeling of soft deep fur, like that of rabbit or hare, against your skin on a cold day is delightful. A rabbit pelt is made up of thousands upon thousands of fine hairs that trap body heat, providing the rabbit with a thermal layer of insulation second to none. The insulating properties of rabbit fur far outstrip the capabilities of a manmade fabric, so when you use the rabbit pelt to make garments for yourself you have clothing that provides an unbeatable level of warmth. It is not by chance that people living in Russia wear coats, hats, gloves and boots either lined with or made out of fur.

When it comes to insulation there is nothing man can produce that beats the thermal properties of down – the under-feathers from a bird – and if you butcher sufficient numbers of birds you have access to enough down to make garments and quilts. Making garments, bed coverings, rugs and other items from skins and from feathers, not only gives you skills and uses up items that would otherwise be thrown away, it also saves you a lot of money.

I have a pair of rabbit skin mittens that I wear daily during the cold weather to do my work around the smallholding, but before I made my own mittens I used to buy gloves that cost about £40 or £50 a pair. However, these gloves would only last me a couple of months, due to the high degree of wear that they received and so it would cost me roughly £100 each year just to keep my hands warm. Gloves are essential in the winter up here in Scotland as the sub-zero temperatures mean that you just cannot work with bare hands in such conditions.

The mittens I made for myself have a fur lining and a high fur cuff that comes right up the forearm keeping out cold draughts, the palm is covered with a layer of waxed, waterproof material taken from an old coat and the back of the mitten has a waterproof nylon covering taken from an old pair of leggings. As you may have gathered, I throw nothing away and neither should you; sooner or later the smallholder can find a use for almost anything. My mittens last season after season and when they do get damaged I simply repair them, as I have the materials they were made from readily to hand. By curing rabbit skins and making my own work mittens, I save myself approximately £100 a year on keeping my hands warm, that's a £1000 saving over a ten-year period.

I also make my own slippers in a moccasin style out of rabbit skins; before I did this I used to buy roughly two pairs of slippers each year, as even good quality slippers seem to fall to pieces after about six months. Slippers are about £20 a pair so I was spending about £40 each year, which is £400 over a ten-year period. By making my own slippers and work mittens, over a ten-year period I save approximately £1500; if you are married, then you and your partner will save nearly £3000.

I am trying to illustrate that, by using every last part of any animal you butcher, there are significant savings to be made to your household budget. We are just talking about the by-products of butchering here, however, if you also add in the amount of money that you save on the meat as well, working on the basis that an average household spends £100 a week on food shopping, which is £5200 a year, without factoring in special occasions like Christmas. If just a quarter of that budget is spent on meat, then the average household spends £1300 a year on meat alone. The home butcher can eliminate this expenditure by using meat taken from the wild for free in the form of rabbit, wild fowl and pigeon.

Raising meat on the holding does have a small cost involved, but this is only a fraction of the cost of meat bought from the shops. So over a ten-year period the average household will spend a staggering £13,000 on meat, whereas the home butcher using meat harvested from the wild, will spend almost nothing and the smallholder raising their own meat will have saved about £10,000. All these savings are only possible if you have the ability to butcher correctly and the skill to use every last scrap of the resource that you harvest.

Another point to make about clothing or footwear made out of skins is that when the clothing eventually wears out the skins, being a natural product, will decompose quickly and harmlessly, unlike manmade fabrics which can take decades to decompose. Fur clothing is also hard-wearing, as demonstrated by garments worn by indigenous peoples hundreds of years ago, many of which have been found still in good condition. So learning to cure skins does not just make economic sense, it is also environmentally friendly.

A FEW WORDS ABOUT FEATHERS

The down from ducks and geese is world famous as the most effective insulating material that you can find and is used in clothing, duvets and sleeping bags. Any product using duck or goose down is expensive to buy, but if you are butchering sufficient numbers of birds you can easily save the down and use it to make the products mentioned above.

An average goose yields about 5 to 6oz (125 to 150g) of usable feathers. These feathers are the softer under-feathers of the body and should be plucked separately into a cardboard box, or onto a sheet of canvas laid on the floor; make sure that you reject any soiled or blood stained feathers. It is quite easy to tell which feathers you want to collect, as they feel soft and silky, whereas the feathers you want to reject will feel harsh. The down feathers should be placed in muslin bags or old pillowcases: do not attempt to wash them, as washing will destroy their insulating properties. Instead, to freshen and sterilize the feathers hang them in their bags in an airy location that is not damp, for example, from the beams in a kitchen or in a spare bedroom.

You want to shake the feathers frequently so that the air gets to them all. When they have hung for four days, tie them up in a pillowcase and sterilize them in a moderate electric oven, at 180 degrees Fahrenheit for two hours. Do not set the oven too high or the feathers will just burn. Once the feathers have been sterilized, hang them again until the odour of duck, which lingers for some time on the down, disappears. This may take as long as a fortnight and again shake the pillowcases regularly to help the feathers to air. You can tell when the feathers are fully aired and ready to be stored simply by smelling them, when the odour of duck has vanished, store the feathers until they are required.

It does not take many ducks or geese to make a quilt and once you have made quilts for everyone in the house you can then turn your attention to duck down waistcoats, pillows and cushions. It obviously takes quite a lot of down to fill a pillow or cushion but if you are taking wildfowl, or slaughtering your own waterfowl on a regular basis, you will soon find yourself with a considerable amount of down with which to make items.

In order to make pillows, cushions, duvets or waistcoats the down must go into a material called ticking, which is a close weave material that prevents the feather end sticking through the material and scratching the skin. When making garments or duvets designed to provide warmth, it is important to make them with

many square compartments, with a couple of handfuls of down going into each compartment before they are sewn up.

If these compartments are not made, all the down will simply end up at one end of the duvet or fall to the bottom of the waistcoat, making the item useless. It is also important not to over-stuff each compartment – a couple of handfuls are sufficient, or in the case of a very large hand, one handful will be adequate. The compartments want to be about the size of the average hand (roughly 4in (10cm) square).

When it comes to the soft feathers of game birds, hens and turkeys, although these are not used to make duvets and clothing, I do not see why they cannot be used to stuff cushions, if they have been sterilized in the same way as duck down. Many cock birds, both domestic and wild, sport the most amazing feathers that are very rich in colour. These feathers can be used by fishermen to make flies for the sport of fly fishing; alternatively, feathers can also be used to decorate the home, simply by placing them in a vase with a few flowers that have been picked from your garden and dried. A skilled flower arranger can make the most magnificent display using feathers.

Feathers can further be used to make feather dusters, which simply involves binding layer after layer of feathers to a thin stick, using a strong fine twine. Again, the feathers used on the duster should be sterilized, to prevent any parasites that might have been on them from spreading to your home. The point I am trying to make is that feathers need not be considered a waste product, they do have their uses and I am still doing more research to find out what the indigenous peoples of the world used to use them for.

CURING RABBIT, HARE OR SQUIRREL SKINS

However, the numerous uses of feathers pales into insignificance next to what can be achieved using the cured skins of rabbits, hares or squirrels (and by squirrel I refer to the grey squirrel, which is considered vermin and not the red squirrel, which is rightly protected by law and cannot be hunted).

There are quite a few books, both old and new, that give rather complex recipes for the curing of rabbit skins (I shall just use the term 'rabbit skins' from now on, but the following information also refers to the skins of other small game as well). I have tried quite a few that require the rubbing of various substances like saltpetre and alum into the skin to cure it. The results of many of these recipes were rather disappointing, producing skins as stiff as iron; so I began to experiment for myself with various approaches, some of which, it has to be said, were a complete and utter disaster.

What I was looking for was a simple method that required little or no expenditure and which produced a supple pelt that would last for many years. Eventually I found that the very best method of all was, in fact, also the most simple and required no pastes, chemicals or expense of any kind. Using this method I have produced pelts that make garments, bags and footwear, all of which last for years.

But before I go on to the actual technique, I want to mention the care of the rabbit in the field, because the production of a quality pelt begins the moment the rabbit is killed. I use wild rabbit skins, but if you happen to raise rabbits on your holding for meat, then the skins of these domestic meat rabbits can also be used. Although they are not quite as dense as the fur you would find on a wild rabbit, the domestic rabbit is a giant compared to a wild animal, so you end up with a much larger skin.

When the rabbit is killed in the field it should not be thrown into the bottom of a game bag, where the fur can become disarranged and blood-stained. The fur may also condensate, due to the residual body heat escaping from the dead rabbit, especially if a number of rabbits have been placed together in the same bag. The rabbit should first be thumbed, a process known as 'peeing', to remove the urine from the bladder, so that it does not leach out and stain the fur. The fur should then be stroked with the hand, from the neck to the tail, to put the entire coat into correct order. If the rabbit is paunched in the field, be careful not to stain the pelt with either blood or the contents of the intestine.

To carry the rabbits from the field, leg them and then place a stick through the legs so that they are carried without interference to their coats. If you are ferreting, hang the rabbits from trees as you work a burrow. When you return home the rabbits should be hung in a dry, airy location, on hooks or nails in a beam. But before the rabbits are hung, inspect them for fleas, which congregate around the rabbit's ears. If fleas are present, use a cotton wool ball soaked in vinegar to remove them; vinegar in which a plant called fumitory has been allowed to distil for a fortnight, is even better than straight vinegar.

If the entire coat is covered in fleas, then skin the rabbit straight away. You then have the option of spraying the pelt with flea spray or burning it. Personally I would not bother trying to salvage a pelt that is heavily flea-infested, for the simple reason that if the fleas are that numerous, the quality of the coat will have been affected. However, I rarely come across rabbits that are covered in fleas; when it does happen, I submerge the rabbit in a bucket of water before I proceed to skin it, as fleas will drown in water.

If you spot the fleas in the field whilst hunting, which is not always possible because some hunting takes place at night, you are best paunching and skinning the rabbit in the field and burying the skin and paunch. This is simply because if you put a flea-infested rabbit into your car, even in the boot, some of those fleas are going to end up in the fabric of your car.

The correct care of the rabbit in the field, or at the point of death, has a direct correlation with the quality of the pelt that you produce, so take good care of the rabbit after death and you will have fur that is very usable. When you are hunting and you return to your car with your rabbits, do not simply throw them in the boot in a heap, but have some kind of set up in your

If the rabbits harvested in the field are not immediately taken back to the car for transportation home, hang them from a tree or on a fence.

When carrying rabbits from the field use a stick, in the fashion shown, or a pony if you have one.

boot whereby the rabbits can be hung from the legs individually. This is easily arranged in four-by-fours and vans but even in saloon cars, with a conventional boot, it should be possible to fashion some kind of arrangement.

Let us now move on to the curing process, as I have already covered the skinning of rabbits in great detail in an earlier chapter. I should, however, mention that I run a fine comb through the coat of the rabbit before I skin it to remove any dirt and loose hairs; you should not do this on your butcher's bench or you will cover it in loose hairs and dirt which is not conducive to good hygiene.

Once the rabbit has been skinned the pelt can be left folded, skin-to-skin, for up to three days in cool weather before you have to pin it to a board. Whatever you do, don't follow the instructions given in some books to rub salt into the skin side of the pelt to preserve the skin; it is not necessary and all that happens is that the salt turns the skin into a wet and slimy mess which takes for ever to dry out, especially in cold weather.

Some people want to wash the pelts and whilst this is acceptable in a commercial environment, where there are specialist facilities and equipment available, the home curer of rabbit skins will make the process very difficult for themselves. If the pelts are washed, they will need to be dried before they can be cured and whilst this can be done, it is by no means easy. I never wash my pelts and they are perfectly clean once they have been brushed; not once have I had any problems with parasites or skin irritations from the skins that I wear.

I should mention that I only cure the pelts of rabbits in their winter coats: in the spring the rabbit will lose its heavy winter coat and put on a thinner coat and the summer coat of a rabbit is nowhere near as pristine as the winter one. This is because in the summer, the does pull great tufts of hair out of their bellies in order to line the nests they make for their young; since the doe has numerous litters throughout the summer, her coat is really quite shabby. The buck's coat is not at its best during the summer

either, because the males are always fighting over the females; buck rabbits are tenacious fighters and will pull great lumps out of one another, which is why you will often find that the ears of mature buck rabbits are torn to shreds.

Pinning the Skins to a Board

1. Once the skin has been removed the next stage is to pin it to a board, which can be a large, flat board or it can be a slatted board, like an old pallet; the only slight advantage that a slatted board offers is that it allows the air to circulate more fully around the pelt. Some people nail their pelts to the board, which is fine, but it is rather a slow method of pinning if you have eight or ten pelts to pin in one go; I prefer to staple my pelts to the board which is extremely quick.

2. The pelts need to be stretched so that they are as tight as a drum: this is best achieved by placing a few staples in the top of the skin, stretching it down slightly and then placing a few staples in the bottom. Now tackle the sides of the skin, one at a time, stretching them as far as they will go. The purpose of pinning the skin is to prevent it shrivelling up as it dries out. The skin should not be placed out in bright sunlight to dry, but should be left in a dry, airy shed. Keeping the pelts out of direct sunlight will prevent them from drying out too quickly and going stiff; you cannot make comfortable garments out of a pelt that is as stiff as a board.

3. When the skins are pinned up you will be able to see fat deposits in the corners. Most books will tell you to remove this fat by scraping it off with the blade of a knife, as soon as the skin is pinned; the reason the fat needs to be removed is because it will eventually go rancid and therefore damage the skin. However, I have found that the fat does not go rancid very quickly, in fact, it can take weeks, sometimes even months (depending on the weather) before

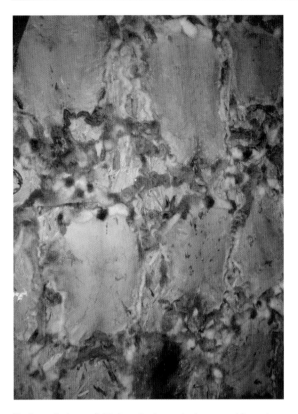

Pin the pelts to a suitable board using a staple gun and then place them in a dry, airy shed, out of direct sunlight to dry slowly.

Both slatted or solid boards may be used and are equally effective; the pelt is pinned skin-side up.

the fat shows signs of rancidity; therefore there is no need to remove it straight away when the skin is pinned. I don't remove the fat as soon as the pelt is pinned to a board simply because, at this early stage, the skin is still somewhat slippery and the fat is not easy to remove; a week later however, the fat has dried and is easy to remove using the side of a knife blade.

4. Once the skins have been pinned, not only do some books tell you to remove the fat deposits straight away, they also tell you to rub the skin with pumice stone or the edge of a knife to remove all the fat and flesh. However, if you have skinned the rabbit correctly, there will be no excess flesh attached to the skin; all attachments to

There are fat deposits in the corners of the skin. Do not try to remove them when the skin is pinned, wait a week or so and the fat will then have dried and can be removed easily.

the flesh will have been carefully removed during the skinning process and there will be no fat, other than the four corner deposits.

When I first tried curing skins I followed the instructions given in the books and rubbed the skins with a pumice stone. However, the result was that the rabbit skins became so thin that they were not durable; now I simply leave them alone. The skins from mature rabbits are thick and have a leather-like quality to them, suitable for using on the soles of slippers. Once the skin is pinned it is simply a matter of leaving it to dry, which, depending on the weather, usually takes about a week to ten days. You can tell just by touching it when the skin has dried out fully: it loses its pliable, almost rubber-like feel and becomes firmer and thicker in texture. Once you have cured a few skins you will soon start to recognize the touch of a skin that is fully dried.

5. When the skin is dry do not waste time prising out each staple, simply take a sharp knife and used the point to cut around the outside of the skin, just inside the staples. I do not remove the staples because it is slow and boring work, but also because the outer edge of the skin will have curled up slightly as the skin dried. This is simply because the staples have to be placed a millimetre or so in from the edge of the board in order to hold the skin, and so the very edge of the skin is not under tension and so shrivels when it dries.

6. Once the pelt is cut out, prise away the edge of the pelt that is left on the drying board, using a pry bar or old screwdriver. Place the pelt on a flat surface, skin-side up and take a sharp knife and use the edge to scrape off the four fat deposits, working from the centre of the skin toward the outer.

7. When the fat deposits are removed I run the edge of the knife over the entire skin, working from the top of the skin to the

Sometimes a pelt is blood-stained on the skin side and some people reject such skins, however, there is no reason to do so. Simply pin them as normal and allow the blood to dry for about a week, then scrape over the stain with the edge of a sharp knife and a thin film of dried blood will lift. The skin beneath will remain blood-stained but it will not smell or decompose. The staining of the skin side of the pelt is not a problem, as this side is never seen.

bottom, in order to remove any fat that has been missed and then rub the entire surface of the skin with a firm brush – a strong nail brush is ideal for the purpose. Then I turn the pelt over so that the fur is facing uppermost and groom it using a strong dog brush; this just gives the fur a final clean and puts all the hairs in the same direction. If you wish, you can sprinkle a cleaning powder over the fur, such as some bran mixed with a few drop of tea tree or lavender essential oil. The skin side of the pelt should have quite a strong leathery smell, but this will die away within a month or so.

To store pelts lay them on a flat surface and put a piece of paper over the skin, then roll the pelt up like a scroll and place it in a sealed box to keep it away from moths. Moths love rabbit skins and if they are not stored correctly will cause havoc among your valuable pelts. For this

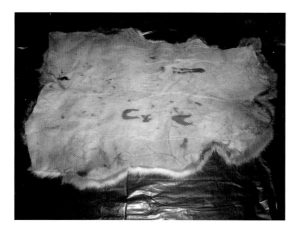

The finished pelt should look clean on the skin side and have a colour somewhere between white and mild tan, although some skins take on a yellow hue.

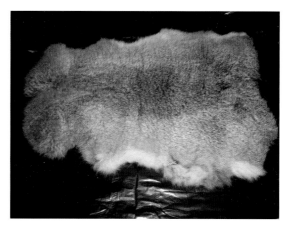

The fur side should look lush and fresh and the hair should be secure, if the hair comes away in handfuls the pelt has not been properly cured or some kind of insect has damaged it.

reason, all garments that are made out of rabbit fur must be stored away during the summer months in sealed boxes. Rabbit skin rugs that are left in the open tend to be left alone, it

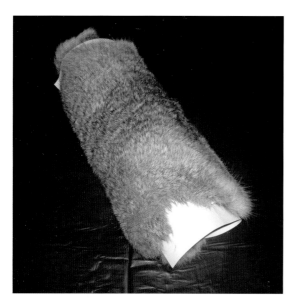

Pelts may be stored for years simply by rolling them up like a scroll and placing them in a sealed box.

is clothing or stored pelts left unprotected in wardrobes or other dark places that the moths strike.

The pelts I produce are green pelts: in other words, they have not been tanned. Many books will tell you that such skins will only stay preserved in the green state for five to six months. However, this is not the case: I have green skins that are years old, they were dried and never tanned and they show no sign of decay whatsoever.

Tanning is a process that involves the application of a paste made up of saltpetre (potassium nitrate), alum and bran that is left on the skin side and then scraped off after a week. I used to tan my pelts using this mixture but I was never very pleased with the results; the tanning always made the pelts much stiffer, making it difficult to fashion garments such as mittens. So I gave up tanning my pelts, preferring to leave them in the green state, which I find much more workable. As you will see from the selection of garments below, the skins of small game animals can be made into a wide variety of useful items that are warm and comfortable and luxurious to wear.

These rabbit-skin extreme-weather mittens are made from a double layer of rabbit skin; they are based on the same pattern as the fur mittens worn by Arctic explorers in Ernest Shackleton's time.

This hat is based on the Russian style and has fold-down ear flaps that will keep the head warm in sub-zero temperatures.

Rabbit fur sewn around the hood of a coat in the Eskimo style, keeps wind and snow off the face and traps in warmth.

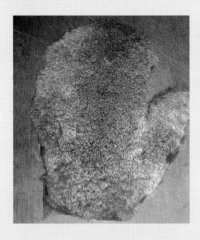

The making of a fur-lined, waterproof mitten.

Suppliers

Humane dispatchers and plucking machines –
Ascott – Tel : 0845 130 6285
www.ascott.biz

Vacuum packing and butchery equipment –
BushWear – Tel : 0845 226 0469
www.bushwear.co.uk

Index

Related Titles from Crowood

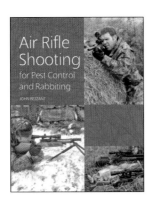

Air Rifle Shooting for Pest Control and Rabbiting
John Bezzant
ISBN 978 1 84797 043 5
160pp, 140 illustrations

Backyard Poultry Keeping
J.C. Jeremy Hobson
ISBN 978 1 86126 958 4
144pp, 90 illustrations

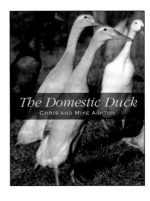

The Domestic Duck
Chris & Mike Ashton
ISBN 978 1 84797 050 3
200pp, 200 illustrations

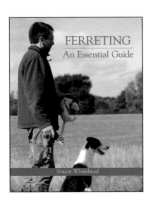

Ferreting
An Essential Guide
Simon Whitehead
ISBN 978 1 84797 036 7
192pp, 140 illustrations

The Pheasant Cook
Tina Dennis and Rosamund Cardigan
ISBN 978 1 86126 376 6
128pp, 8 illustrations

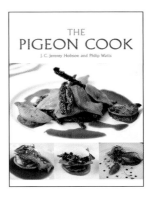

The Pigeon Cook
J.C. Jeremy Hobson and Philip Watts
ISBN 978 1 84797 228 6
112pp, 50 illustrations

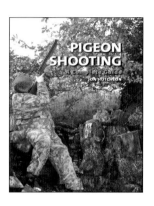

Pigeon Shooting
Jon Hutcheon
ISBN 978 94797 123 4
128pp 90 illustrations

Poultry
A Guide to Management
Carol Twinch
ISBN 978 1 85223 755 4
128pp, 50 illustrations

The Rabbit Cook
J.C. Jeremy Hobson and
Philip Watts
ISBN 978 1 84797 229 3
112pp, 50 illustrations

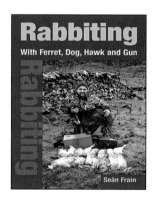

Rabbiting
Sean Frain
ISBN 978 1 86126 802 0
144pp, 110 illustrations

In case of difficulty ordering,
contact the Sales Office:

The Crowood Press
Ramsbury
Wiltshire
SN8 2HR
UK

Tel: 44 (0) 1672 520320
enquiries@crowood.com
www.crowood.com